Our Sweet Maria

Her First 30 Years . . . And Her Final 30 Days

By Jim LaBate

Published by

Mohawk River Press

Mohawk River Press
57 Carriage Road
Clifton Park, New York 12065-7503
518-383-2254
www.MohawkRiverPress.com

All rights reserved. No part of this book may be reproduced or transmitted in any form or by any means, electronic or mechanical, including photocopying, recording, or by any information storage or retrieval system without written permission from the author, except for the inclusion of brief quotations in a review.

Scriptures taken from the Holy Bible, New International Version®, NIV®. Copyright © 1973, 1978, 1984, 2001 by Biblica, Inc.™ Used by permission of Zondervan. All rights reserved worldwide. www.zondervan.com The "NIV" and "New International Version" are trademarks registered in the United States Patent and Trademark Office by Biblica, Inc.™

Cover design by Melissa Worcester and Katrina LaBate. Silhouette from Maria's kindergarten year, 1991-1992.

Copyright (Text and Illustrations) © 2025 by Jim LaBate
First Printing 2025
Printed in the United States of America
Library of Congress Control Number 2024927647
ISBN 9780966210057
10 9 8 7 6 5 4 3 2 1

LaBate explores themes of resilience, faith, and love in a devastating chronicle of the brief life of his daughter. . . An emotional and often powerful tribute.
— *Kirkus Reviews*

With warmth, humor, and insight, Jim takes readers through Maria's struggles and successes from her childhood to her courageous final days. Jim's words radiate a father's love and empathy for his daughter while gently bringing readers to his insightful and comforting reflections on life, prayer, and faith. This beautiful book will bless all who read it.
— Pastor Shad Baker, Pennsylvania

Our Sweet Maria is a poignant and deeply moving account that invites readers into the life of a young family as they honor the milestones of their firstborn daughter—from birth to eternal life. This beautifully written story resonates with anyone who has experienced the profound loss of a child, regardless of age or relation.
— Michelle Payette,
Executive Director,
Beacon of Light Family Ministry, Inc.

No book other than the *Bible* and *Pilgrim's Progress* impacted me more in so many ways than the story of *Our Sweet Maria*.
— Pastor Tim Blanchfield, Montana

Told gently and with an admirable restraint that does not resort to easy sentimentalism, *Our Sweet Maria* is not a story of death but, rather, it is a celebration of life – both earthly and eternal. This book is a love letter to the memory of a much-revered daughter told with heart, humor, and humility by a doting father.
— Tim Kelly, Author of *The Spider Room*

With personal vulnerability and great love, author Jim LaBate gives readers an intimate, at times heartbreaking, portrait of all the days ordained for his sensitive, caring, sweet daughter Maria. In addition, he gives encouragement to grieving people by sharing his family's faith that God created Maria and received her into eternal life. I felt blessed reading this book because I came to know Maria.
— Pastor George Stefani, New York

> "To speak the name of the dead
> is to make them live again."
> Old Egyptian Saying

Thank you to everyone who knew Maria and loved her, but especially to those who are kind enough to remember her and to speak her name.

Other Works by Jim LaBate

Popeye Cantfield — A Full-Length Play

Let's Go, Gaels — A Novella

Mickey Mantle Day in Amsterdam — Another Novella

Things I Threw in the River: The Story of One Man's Life — A Novel

My Teacher's Password — A Contemporary Novel

Writing Is Hard: A Collection of Over 100 Essays

Streets of Golfito — A Novel

A portion of the proceeds from *Our Sweet Maria* will be donated to the American Cancer Society and to Community Hospice.

Dedication

This book is dedicated to everyone who assisted Maria during her final 30 days under medical care. Every single one of you is phenomenal.

From the attending physicians and specialists to the resident doctors, from the registered nurses to the patient care assistants, and from those who delivered the food, to those who cleaned the patients' rooms and hallways, and anyone I may have missed, thank you. You were all patient and kind, understanding and compassionate, and sweet and generous. Your professional abilities and talents are superb, but your human tenderness is beyond belief and well beyond the call of duty.

Thank you. A million times — thank you. We could not have asked for better care for our daughter, and we are forever grateful to all of you. You are truly God's angels doing God's work.

Introduction

When Barbara and I were anticipating the birth of our first child, Maria, I replaced my small, cheap Instamatic camera with my first 35mm camera because I wanted to chronicle all the special moments of our daughter's life. And I did so as Maria first learned to crawl, to stand, to walk, and even to welcome her younger sister, Katrina, who was born two and a half years after Maria. Barbara and I also tried to keep a journal of those early years, but as the girls grew and our lives became even more busy, we stopped writing. And quite honestly, I never expected to write a biography about either girl, but when Maria passed away at the age of 30, I knew I had to write again. This is her story.

In fact, while this book is primarily a biography, it is also partially an autobiography because Maria contributed small portions of it herself. While I wouldn't necessarily describe Maria as a collector, she did like to hold on to pieces she had written, and she often kept journals at various points in her life. Thus, at times in this text, you will see her journal thoughts, her poems, and excerpts from some of her essays.

When I discovered these writings while cleaning out her apartment, I was a bit overwhelmed at first, but as I read through them, I found the reading — and the subsequent writing about them — to be therapeutic, as if I were spending time with Maria again. So for those of you who knew Maria even a little bit, I hope this book will round out your picture of her, and for those who did not know her, I hope her story will give you an appreciation of our precious Maria and also remind you of the precious young people in your life.

Foreward

Anxiously Awaiting Your Arrival
by Barbara LaBate — Spring 1985

Dear Baby,

What a thrill to be writing to you, our very first baby. When I found out the news about being pregnant, I was ecstatic and could barely hold in my emotions. My initial feeling was one of total joy and happiness, just like I felt the day I married your daddy. I just couldn't wait to tell him our news.

But the feelings about being your mother go deeper than those initial feelings, and I would like to share some of them with you now. I hope this is something you will be able to read and even truly understand some day.

I love children and have wanted one of my own for a long time. My work revolves around children because I sell educational materials to families. When I started doing this work as a single person four and a half years ago, I realized how important my work is because the home is the first and most important school, and parents are the most important teachers children will ever have. Sometimes, I agonized over not having a child of my own and would pray to God that I would meet a companion and eventually start a family. I wanted so much to put into practice what I believed other parents should be doing. Well, God answered my prayers in June 1983. Your daddy appeared on the scene when I least expected him. We were married in July 1984, and I became pregnant in

March 1985. Yes, it is quite a Cinderella story, especially when I thought it would never happen.

I can tell you, Baby, that dreaming about having a baby and being pregnant are two different things. The reality of the news is overwhelming. I was just bursting at the seams with the emotions I felt about becoming a mother. I wanted to tell the whole world I was ready for you.

Or was I? Did we conceive you too soon after our marriage? Can we afford you? Will I be able to handle the demands you will place on me? These questions filled my mind too. Yes, Peter-Maria, as we so affectionately call you while you're still in the womb, I am scared too. But deep down inside, because your daddy and I love each other so much and want children, I know we did the right thing. I am ready for you, and the more I'm around babies and children, the more I am convinced. God knew when to send my husband to me, and He knows when it is time to have a baby. It is just human nature to be unsure about new things. And I am no exception to that rule.

When I was growing up, I lacked confidence in myself. I was easily intimidated by people and didn't believe I could achieve in school. My greatest fear was believing I would never meet a man who would love me. I felt I had to be married by age 21, or I would be a failure. What feelings of insecurity I carried around with me wherever I went.

But little did I know that God had a perfect plan for my life. No, His perfect plan and my expectations were not quite the same. I have learned that He knows best always, even if He was off by six years with my marriage plans. Who am I to question? Rather, I am to trust and obey.

My insecure growing years are not something to be looked upon with pity; instead, they should be viewed as a preparation time in my life for my servanthood to God. I was — and still am — being molded, so that I might serve God. During all these years, God was just trying to get my attention to make me realize what is truly important in life.

And so, little Baby, I hope you will gain something very important from my catharsis with you. First, know that I love God, and I rely on Him every day. Second, know that I intend to teach you all I know about God, so that you may have all the confidence you will ever need to live the life He has planned for you. As His Word tells us in Proverbs 3:5-6, "Trust in the Lord with all your heart, and lean not on your own understanding; in all your ways, acknowledge Him, and He will make your paths straight" (New International Version).

I trust in God with all my heart and thank Him for the blessing of your presence in our lives. And with all my heart, I anxiously await your arrival.

Saturday, December 21, 1985 — Happy Birthday, Maria

Dear Maria,

You're so beautiful, and your mother and I are so happy. We're both so excited. I want to write it all down for you, so that someday, you can know the excitement we felt when you arrived, and, also, so that we won't forget any of it.

At about 4:00 p.m., yesterday, we knew you were preparing to arrive because your mom, Barbara, experienced her first contraction. She was making an early dinner, and she felt that she needed to lie down. I finished cooking the macaroni and the ground beef, I set the table, and then we ate. Barbara experienced her second contraction about 30 minutes later, so we both knew that these were your signals for us to get ready to go to the hospital. We didn't have to leave immediately, since the contractions were so far apart, but we had to get everything together to be ready at any time.

After supper, we began a game of Monopoly to relax and to pass the time. Your mother was slowly driving me into bankruptcy when the contractions became more intense around 9:00 p.m. At that point, we switched to watching television. We watched a Christmas special followed by *Miami Vice* and the local news. By midnight, the contractions were about eight minutes apart, so we called the hospital. They suggested we wait until the contractions were close regularly for at least an hour. We did the breathing exercises for each contraction, and between each one, I got dressed to go, I packed the car, and I tried to stay calm — not an easy task. By 2:00 a.m., we both felt it was time to leave, so we drove down the nearby interstate to the hospital where Barbara would deliver you into our world.

During the drive, Barbara felt a few more contractions, and I tried to stay close to the speed limit. I drove carefully through one red light, and we arrived safely within 20 minutes. Your mom was so cute. After we parked the car, I held her hand and carried her bag as we walked toward the hospital's front door. Snow was falling lightly, the outside lights illuminated the baby statue in the center of the circular drive, and we were taking our last walk as a family of two. At that point, Barbara spoke quietly in disbelief: "We're going to have a baby!"

You did not arrive as quickly as we thought you would, however. The nurse examined your mother and told us we still had a while to go. That same nurse directed us to a labor room where she monitored your heartbeat and the contractions for an hour. By the time all these activities had been completed, daylight was approaching, so they gave Barbara some morphine to help her sleep. They knew she would need some rest in order to be strong enough to welcome you into the world later on. While Barbara slept, I went upstairs to wait in the lobby. They suggested I go home to sleep, but I did not want to leave you two. I was sure you were going to arrive any minute, and I didn't want to miss that special moment. I slept in a living-room style chair for about an hour and a half, and, then, I ate my tuna sandwich for breakfast. Later, I tried to read, but I was simultaneously too tired and too excited.

The nurse called me back to Barbara's room at around 8:00 a.m. Barbara felt strong enough at that point to take a shower, so while she refreshed herself, I ate my carob-covered raisins and malt balls for energy. I was definitely ready. Your mom ate a breakfast of toast, juice, and a cup of bouillon. During the remainder of the morning, we moved through the contractions rather easily. Barbara practiced her breathing exercises while I rubbed her back to try and relieve the pressure. Still, the contractions were not coming at regular intervals; they were anywhere between five and ten minutes apart. And between contractions, your mother was amazing. She felt good and strong, she was smiling and laughing, and she was even making jokes and wisecracks. I was stunned to see her in pain one second and laughing the next.

By noon, the contractions were closer and more regular. By then, we were both hungry again, so the nurses brought us lunch: toast, soup, and juice again for Barbara, but I got a delicious piece of chicken and a salad. Unfortunately, I ate it all too quickly between contractions because I was still convinced that you would arrive any second. I was wrong again.

By midafternoon, the contractions were much more intense, and they arrived much more frequently. They gave Barbara an intravenous to make sure she got enough fluids in her body, and, later, they gave her some drugs to help deaden the pain. By 4:00 p.m., they asked me if I wanted to order dinner.

In disbelief, I asked, "Are we still going to be here?"

They said we would, but my hunch was right this time. They delivered the food at 5:30, but we didn't get to eat it. They wheeled Barbara into the delivery room, and they sent me to a special room to change and get scrubbed up. You were finally ready for your grand entrance.

Bonnie, Barbara's nurse, was with Barbara, and Barbara's doctor joined us within ten minutes. Your mom was super. She really suffered as she pushed, and she worried that she wouldn't be strong enough to push you out; however, once she saw the top of your head appear, she found all the strength she needed, and at 6:06 p.m., you officially arrived. You beautiful, little girl, you.

Immediately, the doctor wrapped you in a warm blanket, and she gently set you in your mother's arms. Barbara was ecstatic! Next, the doctor cut the umbilical cord, and you were alive on your own. You were wiggling and crying, and your mother and I were pretty much doing the same things. The nurse then washed you off, and, finally, I got to hold you. I had never held anyone as small as you before, and I was extremely nervous, but by then, you had stopped crying, and you appeared perfectly content. So was I.

I love you, Maria.

Dad

Maria was with us for a full 30 years, but during her final 30 days, she really suffered before she went home to be with her Creator. This book is both a summary of those 30 years and a diary of those final 30 days.

Our Sweet Maria — Her First 30 Years

1986 — Maria's First Full Year

Barbara was 26, and I was 32 when we met on June 7, 1983. We both felt we were getting old and starting to wonder if we'd ever meet someone special and have a family. Thus, when we began dating, our relationship moved rather quickly. We became engaged on New Year's Day, 1984, married on July 28 of that same year, and conceived Maria within eight months. She was born just before Christmas on December 21, 1985.

From the time of Barbara's first contraction until the actual delivery, 26 hours passed, so we were both exhausted, but when Maria finally arrived, Barbara and I were both ecstatic and rejuvenated. Our new life together had begun. I remember feeling so stiff and nervous as I held our precious baby for the first time.

During Barbara's pregnancy and Maria's early years, we kept a joint journal of the experience. We recorded our excitement and our nervousness, and we so enjoyed the beautiful gift that God had given us. Here are some of the details and memories from that first full year with her.

One of the things we did for our Maria was to have her "dedicated" at the non-denominational Christian church that we attended at that time. During the dedication ceremony, we brought Maria forward during a Sunday service in mid-April, and we publicly promised to raise her in a strong Christian environment. In return, the other members of our church congregation promised to help us in that task as much as they could. This church emphasized dedication over baptism when the child is young, so that the child could make his or her own decision about baptism later on when it would have so much more meaning. And 17 years later, Maria actually followed through on that plan by making her own decision to be baptized.

During Maria's first year, we lived in a second-floor apartment in a huge rental complex. I was teaching high-school English at a small Catholic school, and Barbara was selling encyclopedias on a part-time basis. Barbara was also breastfeeding Maria during that first year, so when Barbara had an evening appointment, I stayed home with Maria and tried to feed her the breast milk that Barbara had pumped earlier that day. Unfortunately, Maria would not take that milk from a bottle.

As a result, when Maria got hungry, she cried to me for food and cried again when I did not have the milk she preferred. And when she was hungry, the only activity that calmed her down was when I carried her and walked throughout the apartment. Consequently, on some nights, I would walk for 30 to 60 minutes through the apartment trying to keep her content until Barbara returned. I'd start in the living room, walk into the office at one end of the apartment, then walk back into the living room and down the hall into the kitchen and the two bedrooms before returning to the living room again to start all over. Though I thought I was in pretty good shape at the time, I was always exhausted when Barbara finally arrived.

As Maria began to grow, I often played on the living-room floor with her, and she gradually learned how to roll over and crawl. As she became even more mobile and more playful, we watched her crawl from one end of the apartment to the other and even out into the hallway when Barbara was talking to our next-door neighbor, Natalie.

Maria also seemed to enjoy a bouncing device that we bought for her. It was like a little harness swing that we attached to the door frame between the kitchen and the hallway to the living room. Since she was securely buckled into this device, she was free to bounce a bit and get the feeling of standing on her own as she grew and became stronger.

Finally, the one experience I recall most vividly was when Maria would fall asleep in my arms. Putting Maria to bed each night was a bit of a challenge because she liked to be held. If I tried to put her in her crib and if she were not quite ready, she would cry and reach out to me for more time together. Thus, I would hold her and either walk her or sit in our rocking chair with her. Each night was a bit different in terms of the time needed, but when she finally let go of her tears or her exhaustion, I experienced such a lightness and such a warm sensation, that even though I could put her down at that point, I didn't want to let go of that special feeling. Thus, whether I was walking with her or sitting in the rocker with her, I would often just hold on and experience a tender silence, a silence that American poet Edgar Lee Masters (1868-1950) once described as a "deep peace of mind" ("Silence"). In fact, I experienced that silence so often during Maria's first year, that eventually, I put words to my feeling, and I wrote this short poem to her:

Sleeping in My Arms

From the mountains to the valleys,
From the cities to the farms,
Nothing is more soothing
Than you sleeping in my arms.

You can silence all the cannons,
Turn off all alarms.
Nothing is more peaceful
Than you sleeping in my arms.

I'd give up all possessions,
All money, luck, and charms
To experience this moment
With you sleeping in my arms.

Years later, when we told Maria these stories, she seemed to enjoy them, pleased perhaps to know that we cared enough about her to comfort her, to protect her, to entertain her, and to allow her to grow during that crucial first year of her life.

1987 — Move from Our Apartment to a Townhouse

Just prior to Maria's first birthday near Christmas at the end of 1986, Maria began to stand and hold on to the coffee table. Thus, as nervous, new parents, Barbara and I worried that Maria might crawl under a full-size Christmas tree and pull it over on herself. So, instead, we decided to buy a small Christmas tree and set it on a table, which worked out fine.

What happened instead, though, was Maria got her hands on a Christmas tin of cookies, and while we weren't looking, she somehow pried off the top of the tin, and the cookies flew everywhere. While the moment was likely surprising and frightening for Maria, Barbara and I thought it was precious and hilarious.

Soon afterwards, in January 1987, Maria began to stand and walk on her own. At that point, Barbara and I realized we wanted more room for her to play, both inside and out. The apartment complex where we lived had only a small playground, and because we lived on the second floor, it always seemed like such a big project to get ready, go downstairs, and then hike over to the playground, so Maria could go on the small slide and swings. We began to wonder, "Wouldn't it be nice if we had our own place with a swing-set in the backyard?" Thus, about halfway through Maria's second year, we found a townhouse to rent.

The townhouse was a two-floor, three-bedroom, end unit on a cul-de-sac. We loved it because some friends from church gave us their old swing-set and helped us to place it right outside our back door. We also had a big side yard and multiple neighbors with kids. Though Maria wasn't yet big enough to really interact with most of those kids, she did enjoy playing in our little, green, turtle sandbox and splashing in our small, plastic swimming pool.

I also remember other small moments in that townhouse.

While Maria had learned to walk by the time we moved in, she wasn't quite ready to walk up the stairs to the second floor on her own. Rather, she crawled from one step to the next to go up, and she slowly slid on her tummy, feet first, to go down. Adorable.

I also recall that when she was too tired to walk or crawl, she would look at me, raise her arms high, and simply say, "Up! Up!" Naturally, I picked her up and held her close to my chest, and when I did so and she wrapped her tiny arms around me, I felt like she picked me "up" as well.

Finally, I remember regularly saying, "Good night" to Maria in that townhouse. By then, of course, she went to bed more easily, but after we put her in her crib each evening, and after Barbara and I went to bed as well, Maria would say, "Night" to us from across the hallway. Then, either Barbara or I would also respond, "Night." Then, Maria would say, "Night" again, and we would do the same. This would go back and forth at least a dozen times — and sometimes many more — before Maria would finally start to get tired, and her farewells would slowly begin to fade before we could all go off to sleep. What a sweet and wonderful memory of this sweet and innocent child.

1988 — Katrina's Birth

Maria, naturally, became so much more physically capable during her third year. She began to dress and undress herself at the beginning and end of the day and at other times when needed, and she was very independent about it. If Barbara or I tried to help her, Maria resisted because she wanted to do it all by herself. Only when she got stuck for some reason did she cry out for help.

Also, we gave Maria her first big chore during her third year. In our living room, we had a big set of drapes that covered the windows on the side of the house. Naturally, we opened these drapes first thing in the morning and kept them open until it got dark outside in the evening. Once Maria figured out how to tug on the cord to open and close the drapes, she immediately wanted to do it over and over again. Fortunately, she understood quickly that we only needed them opened and closed once per day, and she was happy to perform that task for us.

Naturally, too, she began to assert herself and challenge her mother and me at times. For the most part, when she misbehaved or challenged our authority, we disciplined her by giving her a timeout on the living-room couch. According to one of Barbara's journal entries in September, she had to put Maria on the couch "three or four times" in one morning alone.

Also, during dinner, Maria sometimes wouldn't always eat her food when we ate. When that happened, we left her food on her plate, and we allowed her to eat it later when she was ready. At some point during the evening, however, I would clean up, and once that happened, I put all the food away, and she could no longer eat. On one particular night, though, I was putting her in bed and getting ready to turn off her light, and Maria felt hungry and remembered her food, and with her saddest little face she said, "I so hungry, Daddy; I want my macaroni." I have to admit, I really wanted to cave in and feed her, but I also knew that wouldn't help her realize that she needed to eat during dinner time, so I stayed and talked to her a bit more until she fell asleep, empty stomach and all.

That food request reminds me of all the many other cute things Maria said as she became so much more verbal; by the end of the year, she was talking up a storm. Early on, she said "googa" for "good" and "noah" for "no." When we spent time with Barbara's sister's family, Maria said "Ra" for her cousin Russell and "Inda" for Aunt Linda. Also, she often said "minute" for "wait a minute." For example, if I wanted her to put on her shoes in the morning, but she hadn't yet hung up her pajamas, she would say "Minute" and hang up the PJs first. She also said "I helpa" when she wanted to assist Barbara or me. At times, too, she combined words as if they were one, and she drove Barbara crazy by asking her often "Whatareyoudoing?" Finally, during her evening prayers, Maria regularly said, "I love Mommy, I love Daddy, and," by emphasizing the syllable "my," she would finish with "I love MYself." Adorable.

Besides her own physical changes, Maria also had to adjust to some changes in our family because our second daughter, Katrina, was born in June. To prepare for Katrina's arrival, we moved Maria from the crib in the nursery to a "big girl" bed in our third bedroom. This was problematic at first because Maria fell out of that bed three of the first four nights and, not surprisingly, wanted to go back to the crib. To correct that problem, we bought a bed rail for her, and she adjusted.

We also hoped that Maria would be out of diapers at age two and a half when Katrina arrived, so we encouraged Maria's toilet training by placing a chart on the wall of the downstairs bathroom. Every time Maria went to the bathroom on the toilet, she got a big star on her chart. She loved those stars, and pretty soon afterwards, she no longer needed her diapers.

Finally, to help prepare Maria emotionally for Katrina's arrival, we talked to Maria often about the coming baby as we took Maria to all of Barbara's medical checkups and also brought Maria to a sibling class at the hospital where they explained what was about to happen. Maria was one of the younger children present, so I thought she'd want to sit on my lap, but she willingly sat with all the other children, and she comfortably held the baby doll that they passed around to give her the feel of holding this new baby.

Also, during those long waits in the doctor's office, Maria enjoyed playing with an Etch A Sketch that was available for the children. Since she enjoyed that toy so much, Barbara and I bought one for Maria and gave it to her as a gift from her little sister when Katrina arrived. Then, when I brought Maria to the hospital to see Katrina for the first time, Maria noticed that all the other babies had a teddy bear in their cribs with them, so Maria insisted that we bring one for Katrina on our next visit. What a great big sister.

1989 — Three-Year-Old Nursery School

During Maria's fourth year, she wavered quite a bit on the edge between being tentative and fearful, especially in new situations, and then becoming confident and comfortable later on. For instance, when we brought her to the doctor for her three-year checkup, at first, she actually tried to run away from the doctor, but by the time the whole experience was over, she was able to speak directly to the doctor and say, "Merry Christmas!"

Similarly, when we arrived at my sister Marie's house to celebrate Christmas with my family, Maria was afraid of my sister's cat and wanted nothing to do with it. Later in the day, however, after she had become accustomed to the cat's presence, she was willing to pet the cat and actually wanted to bring the cat home with us.

Naturally, I saw other examples of Maria's hesitancy throughout the year: wearing swimmies for the first time in the pool, visiting the nursery school she would attend in the fall, and experiencing a Christian summer camp in the Adirondacks for the first time. In each case, Maria was frightened or overwhelmed by the newness of the situation, yet she gradually adjusted, overcame her fears, and settled in comfortably. What a blessing it was to watch this sensitive young girl grow just a little bit during each of these experiences.

The camp was extra special because it was a brand new experience for all of us and the first little vacation we had with the four of us. This Christian organization — Young Life — ministered to high-school students, and Barbara and I decided to be financial supporters. As a result, we were invited to visit the camp as a family on the weekend before Labor Day, so we could see and experience first-hand what the ministry offered to students. The experience was phenomenal because we were joined by many other supporting families, and we spent four days in the Adirondack Mountains in upstate New York, enjoying the beauty of God's creation on a beautiful lake.

    The housing situation was a bit tricky because Barbara and the girls had to stay together in the girls' dormitory with about eight other females in a big room with bunk beds while I stayed with another dad and his two boys in a smaller room in the boys' dormitory. Other than the separate sleeping quarters, though, we spent most of our time together as we shared group meals in the dining hall, splashed in the water at the beach, created artwork in the craft shack, and experienced riding together in both a canoe and a motorboat for the first time. Then, each evening after dinner, we also enjoyed songs, games, and entertainments that were all centered on Jesus Christ and the importance of His role in our lives.

    That first year at Young Life Camp was pretty overwhelming for all of us, but we were fortunate to attend again for three or four more years, and I so enjoyed watching both Maria and Katrina become more and more comfortable and more and more interpersonal and independent each year. I like to think that those special times helped to create a firm foundation of experiencing God's love and power in a new and different way, one that would help the girls grow and mature socially, emotionally, and spiritually during the years to come.

Consequently, Maria began to assert herself. Previously, she was very clingy when we went to the playground or visited other families. She always wanted to be right next to Barbara or me, so she would feel safe. But the more we went to the playground or visited others, the more Maria began to move out on her own. She began to go on the swing set or the slide by herself, and she began to play more easily with other children. She became more independent and began to think of others. For instance, on my mother's birthday, Maria sang for her.

Then, at another time when we went for a walk in the neighborhood, Maria noticed that one of the nearby girls had left her bike at the small playground on our street. I told Maria that we would pick the bike up on our way home and return it to her. However, we returned home by a shortcut through the woods, and I completely forgot about the bike. Maria did not. She reminded me of it, and together, we returned to that spot, retrieved the bike, and brought it to the girl's house. I have to admit I was so impressed and proud of her at that moment.

Generally speaking, too, Maria was usually so obedient. One time, she refused to enter a neighbor's home when invited because she said she had to get our permission first. In another instance, Maria watched from our driveway as all the nearby kids were playing in the circle of grass at the center of our small court. Naturally, they invited Maria to join them, but again, she said she could not leave our driveway until we gave her permission, and until that happened, she just watched and waited.

Was Maria perfect? No, of course not. As she grew, she began to test us a bit. I remember one time when she lied to us. Barbara and I sat at the dinner table and watched as Maria dipped her finger in a bowl of grated cheese and licked it off her finger. Then, when we corrected her, she denied the action even though we could still see the remaining cheese on her lips.

On another occasion, one of Barbara's old friends, Kathy, came to visit us, and Maria became upset because we were giving all our attention to Kathy. In fact, she wanted Kathy to go home. Even later, when Barbara and Kathy prepared to go out on their own for a bit, Maria was determined to go with them. When we explained to Maria that she had to stay home with Katrina and me, Maria got so upset, she could hardly talk. Naturally, Barbara explained to Maria that what she was doing was wrong. As Barbara did so, she said something that she would explain periodically whenever Maria began to misbehave: "We may not love your bad behavior, but we always love you."

Finally, Maria was always such a good big sister to Katrina. During the summer, for example, Katrina got tonsilitis. As a result, she was somewhat lethargic and crying a lot, and Maria was always right there trying to comfort her. About a month later, Katrina was being cranky because a new tooth was breaking through, but we noticed that she felt better when we distracted her by going to the playground. Again, Maria was right by her side to help Katrina get on the see-saw or climb the ladder to the slide. Then, in October, Barbara went on a women's retreat, so Maria, Katrina, and I were at home and taking care of ourselves: making meals, eating, and cleaning up afterwards. As we worked, I noticed that Katrina was imitating everything that Maria was doing such as setting the table or putting dishes in the dishwasher. Even when the two of them were playing separately, Katrina just seemed more content when her big sister was nearby. As a second child myself, I know the advantage of having an older sibling "pave the way," so to speak, and Maria was so good at that, always looking out for her younger sister.

In September, Maria began to attend nursery school two mornings a week, Tuesday and Thursday. Since Maria was born in December 1985, she missed the local September cutoff date for starting school the previous year, and she was almost four by the time she began nursery school. As a result, she was one of the older students in her class. Despite Maria's growing confidence that year, she was a bit apprehensive about this new adventure, primarily because she would be away from Barbara for a few hours at a time. Fortunately, the nursery school had excellent, experienced teachers who had seen similar behavior before, and they welcomed Maria warmly and encouraged her and Barbara to make the transition at their own pace.

In addition, the head teacher at that school was an accomplished pianist, and she used music and singing quite often to instruct the children, activities that Maria really enjoyed. Maria also made a good friend that first year, and that friend also had a younger sister who was about the same age as Katrina. Consequently, Barbara and our girls and the friend and her mom and sister would sometimes get together for lunch after school or for play dates, and the dads were included a few times after work as well. Thus, Maria's new friendship had allowed us to make new friends, a special experience that I hadn't really anticipated beforehand. Unfortunately, that family moved away soon after Maria and her friend completed their second year of nursery school over a year later.

1990 — Four-Year-Old Nursery School

For a week in mid-July, evangelist Billy Graham came to our area for a Crusade at a nearby arena. Both Barbara and I signed up to help out as much as we could as an usher, as a counselor, or as part of the follow-up team. As a result, we were in the arena two or three times that week to hear Reverend Graham speak, which was amazing, but even more amazing was what Maria did during that week. Despite the fact that she was less than five years old, one night when Reverend Graham issued a call to those in the audience to come forward if they wanted to give their lives to Jesus, Maria asked Barbara if it were okay to do so. Barbara was surprised, but she said, "Yes" and accompanied Maria to the arena floor where Maria also spoke to one of the counselors and confirmed her desire and willingness to give her life to God. Did Maria fully understand what she was doing at that early age? Most likely, she did not. However, in some small way, God had obviously touched Maria's heart, and she responded in kind. Naturally, Barbara and I were both so amazed and yet so proud, and in subsequent years, we would see many examples of God's presence in Maria's life. Thank you, Lord.

    In September, Maria began her second year at the same nursery school she had attended previously, and she had the same teacher. The only real change for the four-year-olds was attending three days per week instead of two. Thus, Maria experienced no struggles, and she loved going to school on Monday, Wednesday, and Friday mornings. Looking back, I sometimes wonder if those early years helped to instill in Maria her love for learning and her later desire to become a teacher herself.

    Another educational activity that began that fall for Maria was her piano lessons. I don't remember exactly when, but at some point during the summer, a family in our neighborhood asked us if we wanted an old, upright piano. I don't think we had previously talked about having a piano in the house for the girls, but when the opportunity for a free piano presented itself, we agreed it would be good to have it, and, perhaps, the girls would take lessons at some point. Since I had taken piano lessons for over two years as a young boy and since Barbara had played guitar in high school and college, and, in fact, still owned a guitar, we agreed to move the piano into the townhouse to help expose our daughters to the musical world.

    Then, when we began to think about lessons for the girls, we realized a woman in our church taught piano, and when we expressed some interest, she invited us to her home for a free workshop she was offering on the Suzuki method of teaching piano. Neither Barbara nor I had ever heard of that method before, and we assumed that our girls were too young, but this woman convinced us otherwise.

At the workshop, we learned that the Suzuki method was a relatively new method of teaching music, and the presenter explained how learning to play an instrument was similar to learning how to speak one's native language. This method encouraged an early start, extensive listening, memorization of the pieces, and, of course, regular practice, ideally with a parent nearby. In addition, the supervising parent wouldn't just drop the child off for the lesson, but, instead, would sit, observe, and take notes. One newspaper writer described the method as "Mom Centric."

In our case, since I had more piano experience than Barbara, the method became "Dad Centric." I should have realized that might be a problem because when I took lessons from ages ten to 12, I hated practice and was never very consistent. Consequently, my teacher eventually dismissed me. (A long, pathetic story, believe me.)

In Maria's case, though, she did pretty well. Though she wasn't perfectly disciplined, and though I had to remind her often to practice, she played much better than I ever did. In fact, she took the Suzuki lessons for over two years and played in three end-of-year recitals. In April 1991, she played two folk songs: "The Honeybee" and "Mary Had a Little Lamb." The following May, she played "Mary Had a Little Lamb" again plus another folk song called "Lightly Row." Then, in 1993, in her final year of using the Suzuki method, she played two more songs: "Goodbye to Winter" and "Little Playmates."

In subsequent years, Maria switched to a more traditional form of piano instruction and took lessons from a few different teachers. As a result, Maria got to the point where she played at some family gatherings, she played at the graduation ceremony of a daycare facility where Barbara worked, she participated in a few competitions, and she even gave lessons to a younger girl who lived in our neighborhood. In fact, after Maria passed, that young neighborhood girl sent us a sympathy card, and she recalled those lessons: She wrote, "I will always remember Maria giving me my first piano lessons and how she used to babysit us. She was so patient and kind to us."

1991 — Afternoon Kindergarten

Near the end of our annual lease on the townhouse, our landlord informed us that she hoped to sell the townhouse, and she asked us if we were interested in buying it. Quite honestly, we loved that spot because not only was it at the end of a quiet cul-de-sac but also right behind the elementary school that we wanted Maria and Katrina to attend. Unfortunately, we were not yet in a position to buy, so we had to again look for another place. Based on our previous experience at the apartment complex where we first lived, we looked for an apartment there and found one.

Though it was much smaller than the townhouse, we decided to go back to that complex as we continued to save for our own place. The move, while a bit frustrating, was not that disruptive to the girls' schooling because it simply meant that Maria would begin kindergarten at an elementary school different from the one we had anticipated, and Katrina would begin three-year-old nursery school at the same school that Maria had recently completed.

Since our new home only had two bedrooms, the girls had to share one of them. That wasn't a problem because they got along well, and Katrina still seemed to enjoy having her big sister around all the time. One funny memory from that shared bedroom involves a poster of Cruella de Vil that we had placed on the wall.

Cruella is the main character in the Disney movie *The Hundred and One Dalmatians*, a movie that had been re-released during that summer. Somehow, a co-worker had acquired a wall poster of Cruella and the dogs, and because this co-worker knew that we had young girls, she thought we might like to have it. Naturally, I brought it home, and the girls, who had already seen the movie, excitedly helped me hang the colorful poster — with Cruella and about a dozen puppies — on the wall near Katrina's bed.

Unfortunately, at night, with only a little outside light shining in the window, Cruella's mean face on that poster scared Katrina so much that she often couldn't sleep. When that happened, she hopped out of her own bed, ran across the room, and squeezed in alongside Maria on her bed. Unfazed, Maria moved over a bit, put her arm around Katrina, and they fell asleep together. What a pair!

Another advantage of that smaller apartment was its location. Instead of living on the second floor, as we did when Maria was born, our new apartment was on the first floor and much closer to the children's playground. As a result, we spent a lot of time out there, and we soon met four young girls from three different families who lived in that same section of our complex. Thus, the girls had lots of playmates, and one of those girls also rode the bus to kindergarten with Maria in the fall.

And one final funny memory from our first summer in that small apartment involves jello jigglers. Each year around Memorial Day, my brother-in-law Paul and a few other hometown friends organized a camping weekend for dads and kids; no moms were allowed. He had invited us previously, but I felt our girls were too young, and Barbara wasn't quite ready to let them go. By the summer of 1991, though, Maria was five, Katrina was three, and Barbara probably needed a break from us, so she said it was okay. In fact, she eagerly helped us pack and load the car, she made some sandwiches for us, and she even made one of the girls' favorite treats: jello jigglers.

For those who have never tasted these jigglers before, they are, obviously, made out of jello, but they are made in small, easy-to-handle shapes like stars, fish, and circles, among others. These jigglers were packed in the cooler along with the sandwiches and drinks, and we headed out with our small tent for one overnight with four other families camping nearby at a lake about two hours away. I felt one night would be a good test of our camping abilities, and everything went pretty well as far as I could tell. We swam in the lake, we explored in the woods, and we ate our sandwiches for lunch and hot dogs for dinner before we sat around a camp fire later that night. The only problem that occurred went completely undetected by me until the following night when we made it home and went to bed.

Apparently, during our short excursion, with no mom around to supervise, Maria so enjoyed those jello jigglers that for every bite of a sandwich or a hot dog, she also ate a jiggler. That's a lot of jigglers. So at home that next night, at about midnight, she called out, "Daddy!"

Naturally, I ran into the girls' bedroom to see what was wrong. Fortunately, an exhausted Katrina was sleeping in her own bed, so when I got to Maria, she was sitting up, and I said, "What's wrong, Baby?"

She didn't say a word. Instead, she started throwing up jello jigglers all over her bed sheets. At that point, I panicked. Instead of allowing her to finish in one spot, I tried to carry her to the bathroom. Big mistake. Poor Maria continued to expel her jigglers all over me and all over the bedroom floor and the bathroom floor until we reached the toilet. What a mess!

By then, of course, Barbara was awake and had rushed in to clean up Maria and comfort her. Me? I was on my own to clean not only myself but the mess in the bedroom, the hallway, and the bathroom. What a night. We *never* went camping again.

Maria's kindergarten experience (afternoons only) was a good one. She had a wonderful teacher with lots of experience, a woman who communicated well with Maria and with us. Consequently, Maria did well and earned a "Satisfactory +" in all of her academic categories with an extra "Yes!" in two categories of social development: "shows interest and enthusiasm" and "shows confidence." In addition, at mid-year, her teacher commented that "Maria likes to put care and effort in all her activities," and she is a "delight." As her parents, obviously, we were proud of her scholastic progress, but we were even more proud of the way she interacted with others. By the end of the year, her teacher added the following: "She is friendly, polite, and a special friend," qualities that we would later observe in Maria during all of her school years.

1992 — First Grade

After kindergarten, Maria had to switch schools again, not because we moved again but because our school system hosted numerous kindergarten classes in one building on the main campus and then assigned students to different grade schools on that same campus for first grade. Once again, Maria had another experienced, female teacher, and Maria thrived in the classroom. In addition, she thrived for the first time on the athletic fields.

During the late spring, most of the local grade schools hosted a Field Day for all of the students. This day included athletic competitions such as individual races, relay races, and some field events such as the long jump. Maria always seemed to enjoy running and was pretty good at it. I don't remember many details about this day, but I do know that Maria came home with a red ribbon for "2nd Place." That may have been an individual award or a team award; again, I'm not sure. What I do know is that this was Maria's first athletic award and that she hung it up proudly on her bedroom wall and later collected many similar awards not only for running but also for gymnastics. Through the years, she displayed these ribbons either on her bedroom wall or on her dresser, and as she got older, she preserved them in protective plastic sheets. And as her dad, I enjoyed the double benefit of, first, watching her compete and, second, seeing the pride she felt as she received her awards and displayed them for herself and for others.

Unfortunately, the end of that school year was also a bit traumatic for Maria because her best friend from that school year moved to Michigan with her family. Sadly, since we live in a rather mobile, suburban community, this happened to Maria a few times during her grade-school years, so she experienced this loss more than once. By the time she reached high school, she was able to express her thoughts about one of these significant losses. On the next page is the essay she wrote for her 11th-grade history class:

Maria LaBate
September 10, 2002
History Per. 8 Seat 20

An Event That Impacted Me

What is history? History is not simply the facts in history class, but, rather, the events being played out each and every day. History is the daily actions of a person's life. History is not only for the heroes and leaders, but also for every human being on this earth. Each and every day, people are making history. History can often have a significant impact on a person's life. One example concerns me and the move I dreaded.

I was in first grade at my elementary school. This was my first year in that building because I had come from a different school the year before. The most memorable part of first grade was my friend, Katie. She and I were best friends. I remember her coming to my house; I remember going to hers and the birthday party at her house where we all received balloons with clues in them that led to a prize. Unfortunately, that year came to an end. Not only was it the end of a school year, but also the last time Katie and I would see each other. Both of us were moving.

Receiving this news wasn't easy. She went to Michigan, and our family bought a house in another development where I would go to a new school. I lost my best friend, and at the same time, I had to make new friends. I felt extremely sad and remember disliking the change very much. I cried every time I thought of what had happened. As time went on, I was able to deal with the sadness. When school started up again, I used what had happened to me as a building block instead of a stumbling block.

Going to a new school wasn't easy, but by having a good attitude, I was able to enjoy second grade. This change, although hard, led me to make new friends and helped me to deal with change then and in the future. This event has helped me to realize that when God shuts a door, He always opens a window. The next time you feel as if everything isn't going your way, remember to look for the window of hope and make the best of each and every situation.

1993 — Second Grade

As Maria mentioned in her essay, we finally bought a house during the spring of 1993. A mortgage specialist we had spoken to previously called us and told us to look at an article in the local paper. This woman worked for a bank that was offering a special program for first-time homebuyers, and as the article explained, we would not even need a down payment; the full price of the home could be financed as part of the 30-year mortgage. Barbara and I were ecstatic. We began looking immediately, and we found three townhouses that were not only in our price range but also in a neighborhood where our girls would be able to attend the school we had originally desired. Katrina could start kindergarten there, and Maria could begin second grade. After evaluating our choices and after some negotiating, we finally purchased a three-bedroom, end unit with a small yard, a one-car garage, and a full basement. What a blessing from God!

    We were all so excited in June when we moved in, so excited, in fact, that I borrowed my dad's video camera, so we could videotape what the townhouse looked like and show the tape later to our family members who lived out of town. Naturally, I held the camera, and Maria walked me through the house and pointed out each room. Katrina tagged along as well, and the two of them took special pride in their bedroom, the bigger of the two bedrooms at the front of the house, with Maria's bed near the window seat that looked out onto the street. At the time, we kept the smaller, front bedroom as a guest room, but a few years later, Maria moved in there, and together, we painted it pink for her.

    When September rolled around, Maria was especially excited for her first day in second grade at her new school. The school didn't actually seem new to her, though, because we had been so near to that school when we previously lived in the rented townhouse for four years. During that time, we often visited the school's playground, so Maria was familiar with the swings, the slides, and the seesaws. Back then, too, I'm sure we told Maria she might go to school there, so, finally, she was about to go inside.

    On that first day of classes, I still had the video camera, so I was filming as Maria and a few other local children waited at the bus stop with other parents who were also filming or taking pictures. Barbara was holding Maria's backpack while Maria posed for pictures with the other kids when the bus arrived. In all the excitement, Maria hustled aboard the bus and walked inside to a seat near the window, so she could wave to us. Then, as the bus drove off, Maria realized, even before Barbara or I did, that Barbara was still holding the backpack. Maria's excited smile turned immediately into an open-mouthed look of shock and sorrow. Her first day of school was suddenly ruined. No lunch. No paper. No crayons. Nothing. Oh my goodness!

"It's okay, Maria," Barbara screamed after the bus as it headed down the hill. "I'll bring your backpack to school as soon as I can." I doubted Maria could hear Barbara at that point, but Barbara was actually able to drive almost immediately to the school and arrive just as Maria's bus arrived. Disaster was averted, and we had another funny story to add to our family collection — one that was filmed for posterity as well. What a morning!

Once again, Maria really enjoyed school, and her teacher that year did a phenomenal job of encouraging her students to write. She had the students write stories often, and, then, she asked volunteer parents to transcribe those stories into little booklets with colorful, construction-paper covers. The parents also left room in the booklets for the students to add illustrations to their work. Maria loved the whole process, and I think it really helped her to develop a true love and appreciation for writing, an activity that she practiced often by keeping journals and writing creatively. During that second-grade year, Maria wrote — and kept for posterity — 18 booklets. Some of the titles included biographical stories such as "My Birthday," "My Mom's New Bike," and "About the

Dentist" and fictional works such as "The Leprechaun" and "Macho Woman."

1994 — Third Grade

Our first full summer as homeowners was a crazy, busy time — and I thought we were busy *before* we bought the house and took on all the maintenance activities that came with it. Our lives were busy during that time not only because we had two young girls — ages eight and six — and all their school and recreational activities but also because I was teaching writing courses in addition to my full-time job as a technical writer and having trouble saying, "No" to other activities that appealed to me. I was on the Board of Directors at our local library, I served as a deacon at our church, and I was writing freelance articles for the quarterly Young Life magazine. As a result, I wasn't spending as much time with Barbara and the girls as I should have. Fortunately, Barbara and I came up with our own version of "Take Your Daughters to Work Day" to try and correct that problem.

During the summer, I taught two six-week writing courses, Composition I and Composition II, for the community college. Since these three-credit courses were condensed into six weeks, we had to meet two nights a week for four hours per night, from 6:00 to 10:00 p.m. That's two nights per week for 12 weeks when I had to rush home from my day job, speed through dinner, and, then, essentially kiss the girls "Good night" at that point because they'd be in bed by the time I got home. We had to figure out a way for me to spend more time with the girls, especially during the summer when they were not in school.

Thus, we decided that at some point during each six-week session, I would take the girls to class with me. That might sound like a punishment for some, but we turned it into an adventure. Since those summer classes met not in a typical college classroom but off campus in the basement of a local church, the girls each brought a backpack and a sleeping bag with them, so they could do one of three things: they could sit in the corner and watch the class in action, they could quietly entertain themselves, or they could cuddle up and go to sleep. They loved it — and so did I.

On each of those special nights, we got to spend 20 minutes in the car together before and after class, they got to see what kind of work I did for a living, and they got to stay up later than they would have if they stayed at home. In addition, during the 20-minute break, at about 8:00 o'clock, we always drove to a nearby convenience store where they each got to pick out a drink and a treat to help them through the second half of the class. As I recall, Maria typically enjoyed an apple juice with a bag of Combos, pretzels with cheese inside, while Katrina liked chocolate milk with a bag of M&M's.

Typically, the first half of those classes was a discussion of the assigned readings, so I couldn't always see what the girls were up to, but during the second half, the students and I shared our writing samples with one another, so I usually had time to glance over and watch them. Katrina always brought her Etch A Sketch and her coloring books and crayons, so she was always busy while Maria always seemed to be writing in a journal or just watching and listening before she would drift off to sleep. I sometimes wonder if watching me teach may have inspired her desire to teach as well. In any event, on the ride home, we would sometimes talk about what happened in class or what they had accomplished while sitting in that corner. All these years later, I hope they had as much fun as I did.

    During November of Maria's third-grade year, her physical-education teacher encouraged all of her students to participate in a one-mile fun run, which was part of a local marathon. Naturally, Barbara, Katrina, and I also participated, and we all received small, blue ribbons for our accomplishment. As mentioned earlier, Maria always enjoyed receiving these athletic awards, and she was quite proud of the one she received that year. For this particular award, she filled in the details on the back which included her name and her time: 11 minutes and 14 seconds.

    Maria had another great year in the classroom too. Again, she had a female teacher, but this teacher was a lot younger than Maria's previous teachers, and, thus, she and Maria seemed to connect more closely. Not surprisingly, Maria received excellent grades in *all* of her subjects, but according to her teacher, "Maria loves language arts," and "Her rainforest report on bromeliads is of particular note."

    Quite honestly, I don't recall that report, I haven't come across it in Maria's papers, and I had to use the internet to discover that bromeliads are a colorful, rainforest plant that is related to the pineapple family. Way to go, Maria. Nine years have passed since you left us, and you're still teaching your old man a thing or two.

    This particular teacher also was the most thorough in her description of Maria's schoolwork and her social progress. In two different reports, she described Maria as a "role model," and later in the year, she added, "She sets a lovely example for her classmates." Additionally, she wrote, "She is a delight to have in the classroom, and I thoroughly enjoy working with her." Finally, she added, "Maria is an outstanding child . . . It has been a privilege to work with her. She is a very special person." As a writing teacher, I always told my students to avoid using "too many examples." I hope you can forgive me for doing so in this instance.

    Before I conclude the description of Maria's relationship with her third-grade teacher, I must also describe one challenging event that occurred in our family. That year, Barbara had to be hospitalized for almost a week, so I was a working single dad during that short time. Fortunately, Barbara's situation wasn't life threatening, but the girls, naturally, were worried and concerned, especially Maria as the older of the two. Fortunately, our parents helped out by babysitting when necessary, as did the parents of one of Maria's friends, and Maria's teacher was also a strong emotional support for Maria during that time. I had informed both of the girls' teachers concerning the situation, and while Katrina's teacher was also sensitive and understanding, Maria's teacher just seemed to go above and beyond by talking to Maria often during that week to ease her fears and worries and to ensure Maria that her mom was going to be okay. As a result, I think

Maria was slowly able to pass that confidence down to her little sister. Praise God for those who walk alongside us during those difficult times.

1995 — Fourth Grade

For kindergarten through third grade, I emphasized the fact that all of Maria's teachers were female. That fact probably surprised no one because a large majority of grade-school teachers are female. As Maria's parents, what did surprise us was Maria's reaction to her first male teacher, a reaction that didn't become obvious to us until our first parent-teacher meeting at the end of the first quarter.

During that school year, Maria was in a double class with two teachers, one male and one female. For most of her subjects, Maria had the female teacher. However, for a couple other subjects, Maria had the male teacher, and during that first parent-teacher session, which Maria also attended, he mentioned that Maria was unusually quiet in his classes. When we asked Maria about that observation, all of us — both parents and both teachers — were shocked when Maria stiffened a bit, cast her eyes downward, and began crying. None of us saw that coming. In the ensuing conversation, Maria was gradually able to tell us that she was "afraid" of her male teacher. In one of her later college essays, she described that young fear: "In my eyes, males were stern, strict, and lacked compassion while women were gentle, flexible, and compassionate."

And this particular teacher was one of the nicest guys I had ever met. To his credit, he didn't get defensive or laugh or downplay Maria's fear. Instead, he quickly apologized and attempted to put Maria at ease. Then, we carried on as a group and discussed Maria's progress in her subject matter, and by the end of that meeting, her nervousness disappeared, and she was much more comfortable and relaxed. The rest of the year proceeded smoothly without incident, and on her final report card, her female teacher wrote the following: "Maria has matured both socially and academically," a clear reference to that small hurdle that Maria had overcome earlier that year.

During those early years in grade school, Maria and Katrina both tried various dance and athletic programs. Katrina seemed to really enjoy the dance while Maria really enjoyed the gymnastics. The weekly lessons or practices for these activities were usually about an hour long, and I enjoyed watching the two of them having fun. To keep myself occupied during that time, I always brought a magazine or a book along with me, so it was a win-win for everybody. The final dance recitals and the gymnastics competitions, however, were in another category altogether. In fact, in preparation for these events, I used to joke with Barbara that instead of a magazine or a normal book, I was determined to bring the 1,152-page novel *War and Peace* with me.

I seriously could have used that classic by Tolstoy because those special events were two to three hours long, and they often included the same music played over and over again as the various girls performed and competed, a real test of patience for all the parents. Fortunately, the girls loved every minute, and we have some great pictures of a smiling Katrina in her dance outfits, and Maria collected more ribbons of various colors for her gymnastic efforts. And in Maria's case, the highlight of her gymnastics career occurred on February 9, 1995, when she earned red ribbons for finishing second in the beam and the vault exercises and also earned blue ribbons for finishing first in the bars and the floor exercises which added up to a first-place trophy for "All-Around Champion" for her level and age group. Her hard work and diligence had paid off, and she could not have been happier.

1996 — Fifth Grade

When Maria began fifth grade, we all looked forward to that school year because that would be her final year at her nearby grade school before moving on to middle school, and she and her classmates would be the "big kids," so to speak. Early in that year, though, she filled out a short survey for her teachers that showed both sides of Maria's makeup. On one hand, she wrote, "Two things that make me feel comfortable about being in school are that the teachers help me and because I'm organized." By contrast, she also wrote, "Two things that make me feel uncomfortable about being in school are asking questions because I think people are going to think I don't know anything and because I can't write fast, and I'm always behind." Unfortunately, one of Maria's teachers that year didn't make her feel comfortable, and, as a result, she struggled tremendously.

The co-teachers were a male and a female who shared the instructional responsibilities for two classes of fifth graders. Maria worked well with the female teacher, but she spent most of her time in the male teacher's classroom, and he was a bit too much for her. As mentioned earlier, he was only the second male teacher Maria had during her first six years of school. From what we heard from other parents, this male teacher would always be assigned the most troublesome boys in the class, and he would whip them into shape by being loud and hard and strict, a bit like a drill sergeant. That style may have worked for the boys, but it only made Maria nervous and tense. Years later, Maria described her breaking point in this way:

> One day, he became angry while checking for homework because so many students had failed to complete the task of getting a parent's signature. I, too, had forgotten to do the homework, and when he got to me, he started to yell. I was terrified. I felt as if he were yelling only at me. Due to this experience and others, I felt that he was unapproachable . . . Every Sunday evening, I cried myself to sleep because I knew that when I woke up, I would have to go to school. I wrote notes to my parents begging to be home-schooled.

When Barbara and I read those notes and talked to Maria, she first asked us if we could get her transferred into another classroom. The school authorities said, "No," so Maria asked if we would home school her for the year. Barbara was willing, but I didn't think it was a good idea. I thought it would be good for Maria to persevere and fight her way through it. Looking back, Barbara and I both realize now we should have fought harder for her, either for a different teacher or for the home schooling. We made a mistake, and Maria paid the consequences.

She struggled to eat her meals, she lost weight (on her already thin frame), and, most important, she lost a bit of the joy she had always experienced in the classroom and with her friends. To this day, Barbara and I regret how we handled this situation and regard it as our biggest parenting mistake.

Looking back now at that whole experience, I do think that Maria did gain one real positive from that stressful fifth-grade year. I sincerely believe that as she pursued her own teaching career and worked with students of various ages, I think she became even more kind and sensitive than she had been previously. I think she was determined that no child under her care would ever feel that same humiliation and stress that she endured from that one particular teacher.

Despite that difficult classroom situation, Maria still performed well academically, and she even earned a "Merit Award" in the end-of-year Science Fair. In addition, on her final report card, Maria's female teacher that year wrote the following: "She gets actively involved in lessons and displays confidence and poise when explaining herself."

And despite her weight loss, Maria still continued to enjoy her physical activities at school. Though she no longer took regular gymnastic lessons, she still especially enjoyed her gymnastic classes as part of the physical education program, and she participated in a year-end exhibition at the school. She also participated in the spring field day where she won a third-place ribbon for the long jump. And what was most exciting for me was the fact that she asked me to bring her to school early every day in the spring, so she could be part of a recreational softball program solely for the fifth graders.

    I was excited because baseball was always my favorite sport, but Maria never really showed much interest earlier. Sure, we sometimes played wiffle ball in the grass lot on the side of our townhouse and once per summer at our LaBate family picnic, but that was it. Katrina was usually more enthusiastic about it while Maria seemed to tolerate it for our sake. In this case, though, the school librarian initiated the early-morning program, and he was always kind to Maria, and she liked him. In addition, one of Maria's friends participated, so the whole program was a good fit for her.

    So instead of simply dropping Maria off at school and going to work early, I always stayed and watched for ten to 15 minutes. If I'm being completely honest, I wanted desperately to play too. I wanted to share my favorite American pastime with my sweet Maria. I loved watching her play the outfield using a small glove that her older cousin had handed down to her, and I enjoyed watching her hit and run the bases. No, she wasn't a great player, and she never showed any additional interest in the game, but for one short season, she was my all-time favorite — and she was having fun with her friends. What a blessing!

1997 — Sixth Grade

After Maria's tough fifth-grade year, Barbara used the summer of 1997 to research what we needed to do to home school Maria for sixth grade. Honestly, I still wasn't a big fan of the idea because I had always loved going to school, and I wanted Maria to have a similar experience, but since that wasn't happening, I was willing to give home schooling a try for her sake. Thus, when September rolled around and Katrina began fourth grade at that same grade school, Maria stayed at home instead of taking the bus to middle school. At the house, she studied with Barbara or worked independently with the educational materials we had purchased for her. Maria enjoyed the new experience quite a bit, especially since Barbara had also enrolled Maria — and our family —in a group of like-minded parents in the area. As a result, every Friday, Barbara and Maria traveled to a big local church where they met with other home-schooling families for a morning of special classes or activities. The parents either taught the classes themselves or arranged for local experts to come in and speak to the children. The group had about a dozen sixth-graders, most of whom were female, so Maria developed some really strong friendships. I think that group was especially good because it prevented Maria from being somewhat isolated at home all the time, and it led to experiences that she might not have enjoyed otherwise.

For example, one of the families in the group owned a local apple farm, and they also owned horses. Naturally, we got to know the family a bit, and at one point, when one of their horses was about to give birth, they invited all four LaBates to come over and witness the birth. We arrived at the farm during the early evening, and we sat in their darkened barn for most of the night before the baby horse arrived just before sunrise. What a beautiful and amazing moment to see that young creature come into the world on unsteady legs and begin to walk within minutes. I think we were all speechless and teary-eyed.

Ironically, too, Katrina began to hear and observe so much about the home-schooling experience that by early November, she asked us if she could be home-schooled as well. Barbara was thrilled and couldn't wait to say, "Yes." Again, I was hesitant, but I felt that our family life would be stronger if both girls were schooled together, so I also agreed. Thus, by the time Katrina's school was about to take its Thanksgiving break, Barbara had again submitted the paperwork and secured the necessary books for Katrina to join Maria at home. And that turn of events allowed both girls to take a ten-week writing course in the spring with one of the more famous writers in the entire . . . house.

That's right. I soon volunteered to teach a class for the home-schooling group, and, naturally, both of our girls participated. I was able to offer the class because of another turn of events; I was laid off by my employer, and I didn't find another full-time job right away. Thus, this small group of a dozen writers in fourth, fifth, and sixth grades met in the basement of our church each Wednesday. We covered all the basic writing techniques, and each week, the students had to bring a one-page essay to the group. There, we took turns reading and discussing as many of the essays as we could cover in our two-hour time slot. As I mentioned a while back, Maria had always loved to write for school and in her journals, so this was a new opportunity for her to share her thoughts and ideas with her peers, and she loved it. Did I mention that I loved it too?

During those home-schooling years, our girls also participated regularly in the Christmas and Easter productions at church and the monthly children's messages as part of our Sunday service. Maria was always a bit more of a performer than Katrina. While Katrina was always willing to be an angel or a lamb in the Christmas performances, Maria was more likely to volunteer for a bigger part, one with more lines or the opportunity to sing. One year, for example, she and I performed a short, two-person play about one of the families whose son was executed by Herod after the birth of Jesus. On another occasion, during a family talent show for the LaBate and Zuccaro Christmas celebrations, Maria decided she wanted to sing a solo. So, while her grandparents, her aunts and uncles, and her cousins looked on, Maria sang the following lyrics:

> Christmas isn't Christmas
> till it happens in your heart.
> Somewhere deep inside you
> is where Christmas really starts.
> So give your heart to Jesus;
> you'll discover when you do,
> That it's Christmas,
> really Christmas, for you.

We have that performance on an old videotape, and when we watch it today, we laugh a bit at Maria's sweet ending to the song. She usually sang the first three and a half lines rather slowly, but when she got to the last two words, for some reason, she belted them out quickly and held on to that last note. She was adorable.

One other performance example, out of many, took place when I volunteered to talk about "love" during the children's message one Sunday at church. I asked Maria if she'd be willing to be part of a "Love Jukebox," a device that would require her to stand inside a big cardboard box and sing love songs. She readily agreed, so I secured a box that was plenty big enough for Maria to stand inside (a box that had previously housed a big rocking chair), and we went to work. We designed the outside, so that it actually looked like a juke box, and on the day of the message, I used a small device to wheel it into the sanctuary. Then, I explained to the other children gathered around up front that if we pressed a letter and a number on the front of the box, we could hear various love songs. The children were skeptical, of course, but excited, too, to see what would happen. We even had a bright orange extension cord extending out of the back of the box to plug the juke box in to make it look as if it were electric. Then, as various children chose different letter-number combinations and punched them in, Maria responded from inside, all alone. She sang her heart out too. She sang a line or two from all of the following: "I Love You" by Barney (the big purple dinosaur), "Skidamarink A Dink A Dink, I Love You" by Sharon, Lois, & Bram, and "All You Need is Love" by the Beatles. We were trying to make the point that we don't necessarily need a jukebox to spread the love of Christ. Personally, Maria's willingness to crawl inside that box and perform demonstrated her desire to help her dad talk about love to the children, and that shared endeavor remains one of my favorite memories. Thank you, Maria.

1998 — Seventh Grade

During our home-schooling years, we decided to add another member to our family. No, not another child but a dog. Katrina in particular always wanted a dog, and Maria, though not as enthusiastic, was also excited about the idea and agreed to help Katrina with feeding the dog, walking the dog, and cleaning up after the dog. Neither Barbara nor I had ever had a dog growing up, so this was to be a new adventure for us as well, and we decided to proceed. We felt the timing was right because our home-schooling schedule had more flexibility, and since the girls were older and pretty mature, we were confident that they would definitely do their part. And they did — especially that first year when the dog was just a puppy and pretty frisky.

Barbara found the dog through an advertisement in the newspaper, and this dog was a mixed breed: part Schipperke and part Pomeranian. Quite honestly, we hadn't done much research about dogs beforehand, so we found out later that the Pomeranian half was friendly and playful while the Schipperke half was more of a working dog, a herding dog that was especially popular on ships to find and kill any rats on board. We did know up front that both breeds were relatively small, so we felt a small dog was perfect for our small townhouse.

Since this little dog was black, Barbara suggested the name "Mystic" after Mystic Mints, a cookie we all liked, and the girls agreed. Initially, we all enjoyed this new energy in our home, and we also all enjoyed holding Mystic on our laps when we sat down to watch television in the evening. We even enjoyed, for the most part, chasing after him when he ran out the front door anytime he saw an opening. After a while, though, we tired of that game, and we signed him up for obedience classes with Katrina accompanying him. He failed — miserably. And he took the course twice. Unfortunately, Mystic's lack of discipline — and ours, as well — led to a problem later on for Maria. More on that later.

Home schooling also provided other unique activities for our family. One for me was the opportunity to teach the girls about astronomy. A couple years earlier, I had audited an astronomy course online at our community college, and I was anxious to show the girls the various constellations and the nearby planets. I had them drawing the shapes of the various constellations in a notebook, and, then, we would go out at night and search for them. Naturally, we started with the North Star, the Big Dipper, and the Little Dipper, and we gradually moved on to Orion, Cassiopeia, and others.

In addition, our daily newspaper had a "Night Sky" feature, so when we read that the sky would be filled with shooting stars on a particular evening, we went outside as a family with blankets, pillows, and sleeping bags — not to sleep but to watch the stars overhead. Anxiously, we waited and waited and waited.

Yes, we saw a few shooting stars, but often due to cloudy conditions, those nights of shooting stars were never quite as dramatic as we had hoped. Still today, though, almost 30 years later, I have such fond memories of being outside on the grass with the girls late at night, talking and laughing and wondering about the God who created such a vast and wonderful world for us all. After an hour or so, Barbara or Maria — or both — would gradually fall asleep, a sure signal that our stargazing was just about over for the night. Katrina and I would usually hang on for a bit, hoping to see even more shooting stars before we would eventually wake up our two sleepers and head inside.

Another activity that we all enjoyed was the field trips with a busload of other home-schooling families. For example, I specifically remember the New York City trip. Barbara and I had previously brought the girls to the Big Apple ourselves, once to see the Bronx Zoo and another time to watch the Thanksgiving Day Parade. With the home-schooling group, we added Wall Street, Central Park, and the Metropolitan Museum of Art. Both Maria and Katrina seemed to enjoy "The City" so much more when they were with their friends, and Barbara and I thoroughly enjoyed watching them enjoy the whole experience.

Another field trip brought us to Gloucester, Massachusetts, for a whale watch. That was a long day. Barbara was unable to attend that trip, so she missed the three-hour bus ride and the one-hour journey out to sea. She also missed the rain and the somewhat stormy conditions, conditions that Maria and I did not handle well. Thus, as Katrina sat outside on the deck laughing with her friends in her rain gear and looking for whales, Maria and I huddled inside the cabin, trying to stay dry and warm and trying to keep our lunch down. Fortunately, we succeeded at those tasks, but we never got any real good looks at the whales. For without fail, every time we heard Katrina and friends cheering and screaming for the whales that did appear, we rushed to the windows and only saw the big splashes that followed as the whales returned to the deep waters. Great memory, though.

Finally, during that seventh-grade year, Maria began to take an interest in boys for the first time. One boy in particular caught her attention, but he was rather quiet and more interested in horses and tractors than in girls his own age. Another boy in the home-schooling group was definitely attracted to Maria, and he tried to talk to her periodically, but she was not attracted to him. Thus, Maria began to experience the exciting but also complicated and sometimes frustrating world of male-female relations. Naturally, Barbara and I prayed for both girls regularly.

1999 — Eighth Grade

As a longtime writer, I have written many essays and short stories and submitted them for publication. Unfortunately, the majority of them have been rejected, but every once in a while, I received an acceptance letter, and my work was published. Thus, when we began home schooling Maria and Katrina, as their writing instructor, I was always looking for writing opportunities for them as well. So when our daily newspaper hosted a weekly feature called "Kids' Corner" and asked for book reviews written by children, I encouraged the girls to write a review, and Maria took me up on my suggestion. She wrote about 400 words on a book called *Little Farm in the Ozarks* by Roger Lea MacBride. And her review was accepted and published on June 15, 1999. A week later, she received a check for $5.00. Amazing! I could not have been more excited. Congratulations, Maria!

Later that year, Maria began her eighth-grade year, again as a home-schooling student. As part of her English class, I asked her to keep a journal, and in that journal, she recorded some of her highlights of that year.

She wrote quite a bit about two of her favorite activities: babysitting and teaching. She was 13, and she babysat for a nearby family with a boy and three younger girls. In her words, "I love babysitting them . . . They are a great family."

She also babysat for another young girl who was about four years old, and on one particular day, Maria taught this young girl to tie her own shoes. Afterwards, Maria wrote, "It was so much fun to know that I was able to teach her."

On the other side of the babysitting equation, I'm proud to note that one of the moms who hired Maria for babysitting had this to say about her: "I hope one day when my girls are teenagers, they will shine as brightly for Christ as Maria does."

Maria also wrote about other activities that she enjoyed: her first tennis lesson at a nearby facility, her new piano teacher, driving a golf cart with Grandpa Pete (my dad), and spending time with Grandma

Eileen (my mom), who according to Maria was "just like me." Maria highlighted family celebrations too, such as my parents' 50th anniversary party and Grandpa Rich's 70th birthday party (Barbara's dad). Finally, she also noted how much she liked her outfit for her home-schooling picture and the dress she wore to Pete and Eileen's anniversary party.

Naturally, Maria also wrote about some of her struggles. One daily struggle was her relationship with Mystic. Once Mystic had outgrown his cute puppy stage, he began to assert himself as the herding puppy that he was, and he tried to "herd" Maria often. Sometimes, he chased her up the stairs, and at other times, he nipped at her. We tried to encourage Maria to be tougher with Mystic, so he would know who was in charge, but none of us really disciplined him as much as we should have, and Maria, quite honestly, didn't have it in her.

In addition, algebra was a struggle: Both Barbara and I tried to help Maria with it, but the way Barbara and I had learned algebra a century earlier was quite different from Maria's textbook. Thus, one day, Maria wrote the following: "Today, Mom and I worked on Algebra all morning; we nearly killed each other."

Finally, even the journal, which she mostly enjoyed, became too much at times: "Someday, I'll be glad I wrote this journal, but right now, it seems to be a waste."

Every year, our home-schooling group, behind the excellent leadership of an extremely talented and enthusiastic mom, banded together for two student performances: a Christmas chorus recital and a spring musical. The recital included just about all of the children — roughly 50 to 60 individuals — while the musical involved about half that number.

During this third year of home schooling, Barbara and I suggested to the parents of the group that we also have the students produce a dramatic play, a non-musical, during the spring of 2000. We wanted a play that had numerous parts for the students but also a play that had a pretty simple set. As a result, we suggested the play *Our Town* (1938) by Thornton Wilder. The plan was to have tryouts and some practices in the fall of 1999 and, then, even more practices prior to the actual performance in the spring of 2000. Not surprisingly, Maria, who had always enjoyed performing in our skits at church, tried out for the role of the Narrator, and she was chosen. That particular role has an enormous amount of lines, however, so Barbara and her co-director decided that three other students would share the role. Katrina, too, was hoping to participate.

2000 — Ninth Grade

As a totally biased observer and a heavily invested husband and father, I can tell you that Barbara's directorial debut of *Our Town* was a smashing success, and Maria and Katrina's performances as the Narrator and Mrs. Soames, respectively, were extraordinary. Seriously, they all did a great job and had lots of fun in this spring production. The cast of about

30 practiced every Friday in a nearby firehouse, and we arranged to perform the play at our newly constructed community church.

By June, the end of Maria's eighth-grade year and Katrina's sixth-grade year, Barbara and I decided that we would stop home schooling and, instead, send the girls back to the public schools in September. Quite honestly, though home schooling had been a positive experience overall, I think all four of us were tired of it and ready for a change. While the home-schooling special classes and unique activities were always fun, the day-to-day regimen of doing schoolwork alone at home had become tedious for everyone. By then, too, I had finally secured a full-time job as a writing specialist in The Writing Center at the community college where I had been teaching part-time classes all along. At that point, we felt that Maria in particular was more ready than she had been previously, so she would begin her freshman year at the public high school, and Katrina would attend one of the three middle schools in town as a seventh grader.

Years later, as part of Maria's senior year in high school, her English teacher asked her to write a two-page essay about "a change that allowed her to grow and learn about herself." Maria chose to write about her three years of home schooling. In that essay, Maria highlighted both the positives — "flexibility, more family time, and time to grow closer to God" — and the negatives: "too much free time" (at home) and "not enough time to be with friends" (outside the home). "As a result, I became rather serious and sometimes even depressed because I had nothing to do." Summing up the advantages and disadvantages of her home-schooling years, Maria wrote, "They allowed me to grow up and mature and gave me the foundation that I needed when I returned to the public school." Maria's return to the public school also allowed her to play tennis more seriously.

    Since our family had always played tennis together and since the girls had received some professional instruction as part of a home-schooling special program, I asked Maria if she would like to try out for the high-school team. I think we both felt it would be a good way for her to reintegrate herself into a large public-school setting again, and it worked out beautifully for her. The team tryouts began a week or so before classes, and with the help and encouragement of an extremely kind and gentle coach, Maria earned a spot on the junior varsity team. As a result, she had a half dozen new friends even before the first day of school, and these tennis friends became the core of her social network during the following four years, a network that made it easier for Maria to fit in at one of the largest schools in our area, a school that graduated approximately 700 students each year. In addition, some of the girls Maria had known as classmates in grade school welcomed her back to the public school system, and some of Maria's friends from church were also in the high school with her. Thus, Maria's return to regular school was not at all as traumatic as I worried it might be, and she adjusted quickly and easily. Thank God.

2001 — Tenth Grade

One of the later highlights of Maria's freshman year was attending her first dance in early May. Maria and some of her friends often visited the Clubhouse of a local Christian ministry which was right across the street from her high school. The Clubhouse was an old dentist's office which had been renovated for local teens, so they could have a place to socialize daily after school and sometimes on the weekends. For this particular event, the Clubhouse staff sponsored what they called a "$10 Prom," which meant the attendees could not spend more than $10 on their outfits for the evening — an obvious alternative to the more expensive affairs hosted at the high school. Maria was so excited about the experience that she wrote about it in her journal the following day.

In that journal, she described how she didn't even have to spend a cent on her dress because she borrowed the gown that her Aunt Linda wore when Barbara and I got married, approximately 17 years earlier. Maria even drew a small picture of the gown in her journal, highlighting its bright white color with flashes of bold red at the top and bottom. In her own words, Maria wrote, "It fit great and looked beautiful if I may say so myself."

In her attempt to capture all the details, Maria also described how her friend Jen took 45 minutes to get Maria's hair just right, how everyone ate "ziti, salad, a roll, chocolate cake, and fake champagne" at the event, and how they crowned a King and a Queen of the event based on their outfits. Though Maria didn't win, she mentioned that one of the judges told her later that she was a close second. In her journal, Maria cherished that close call and wrote, "If only they had chosen a Prince and Princess, I could have been in the Court."

During the summer between Maria's freshman and sophomore years in high school, she also had the opportunity to go on a missions trip/work camp in rural Pennsylvania — and I was fortunate to be one of the chaperones. The trip was co-sponsored by our local church and by a national organization headquartered out West. Our church sent ten students and four chaperones, and once we arrived at our destination, we were all assigned to different six-person work teams. I think that was a great experience for Maria because it was her first opportunity to meet and work alongside teenagers from all over the country. In Maria's case, she helped to build a deck on the home of an elderly woman and also to paint the exterior of that woman's home.

In addition, each night, all 400 teenagers gathered in the auditorium of the local high school for a worship service and, later, spent the night with their church team in one of the school's classrooms, using sleeping bags on the floor. While most everyone was exhausted by that time, very few students went to sleep immediately. Instead, they shared their stories from the day and drew closer to one another in the process. Overall, even though Maria was one of the younger participants, she loved the experience and couldn't wait to do it again.

In the fall, Maria again played on the junior varsity tennis team. She was not one of the strongest players, but she loved playing, she was getting better each year, she served as one of the tri-captains, and she looked forward to trying out for the varsity team during her junior year.

As a sophomore, Maria also contributed a poem to her school's literary journal, published in March 2002. I don't remember if she wrote the poem as part of a class assignment or if she just wrote it on her own. In any event, here it is:

If You Could Prepare . . .

The night is clear
the stars shine bright.
You're in your house with innocence
Little do you know of the fire that is to come.

If only you had time
    to select some personal things,
What would they be?
Gold, silver, medals, or
Those things that truly hold life dear to you.

For me, those things would be
My tennis racket, my Bible, and last,
    but not least, photographs, to remind me
    of those who my life revolves around,
    my family.

Later that year, Maria wrote another poem, but this one was directed specifically to Barbara and me for our 18th anniversary on July 28, 2002:

Mom, Dad,

I love you,
You are very good to me.
I love the times in my room with you
    before I go to bed.
You are there for me no matter what —
The good, the bad, the hard, the sad,
    and exciting moments.
May your day be great and many more.
I'm going to be sad when the day comes
    for me to leave,
But I will always love you both
Even when I have my own family.
I love you!

Happy 18th Wedding Anniversary

2002 — Eleventh Grade

Prior to Maria's junior year, she did go on a second missions trip/work camp to Pennsylvania (similar to the first one, but Katrina went on this trip as well), and Maria also served as a student leader at the summer Vacation Bible School at our church. Teaching grade-school children about the Christian faith was something she really loved, and these experiences strengthened her desire to major in education at college.

Of all Maria's high-school activities, however, the one that made me the most happy was her first real job. One of our church families owned an apple orchard, and they sold their produce and other products at a country store that also included a bakery. Maria began working in the bakery about midway through her sophomore year, just after she turned 16, and she continued to work there periodically throughout her junior and senior years as well. So naturally, as Maria's dad, I had to visit Maria — and the cookies, brownies, and muffins — periodically to make sure that everything was okay. In addition, on certain days, Maria was able to bring home older bakery products that hadn't sold but were still delicious. And even when she came home empty handed, she still smelled great — like a freshly made apple pie.

Also during Maria's sophomore year, she passed the written test for her driver's permit, and by the time she was a junior, she had earned her license. The learning process wasn't easy for her, though. She was extremely tentative at first, so, like many new drivers, she practiced in the school parking lot and on deserted roads. I can vividly recall one early practice session when snow was beginning to fall, and even though we were on a lightly traveled, back road, Maria was driving so slowly that everyone was passing her. This made her even more nervous, and by the time we reached our turn to go home, she had frozen — literally. She could not turn the steering wheel, so I had to reach over and help her. Once we turned the corner, I had her pull over, and we switched positions.

Maria took a short break from driving at that point. Once the winter season had passed, though, she was ready to practice again, and after she became comfortable on local roads, we taught her how to get on and off the highway, and we allowed her to drive longer distances. For the most part, she drove well, but she had a tendency to really hug the highway's right shoulder. Since I was usually in the front passenger seat, I had to continually remind her to stay in her lane, and once she overcame this final hurdle, she was ready to take her driver's test, which she passed on her first try. What a day and what an accomplishment! The two of us celebrated by eating lunch outside at a restaurant patio on a beautiful spring day. She was so happy — and so was I.

And by the time Maria began her junior year, she had a car to drive as well. Our neighbors across the street were selling a used Saturn at a reasonable price. Maria and I test drove it, and she was more than willing to use her work savings to help pay for the purchase and for the expenses. Katrina was pretty excited, too, because she knew that as part of the deal, Maria would sometimes have to drive her to and from various activities instead of Mom and Dad. What a thrill! Our little girls were definitely growing up and beginning to experience real freedom. Fortunately, both of them had always been mature and responsible, and Barbara and I felt good about what was happening in their lives.

Once classes started, Maria tried out for the varsity tennis team, and she earned a spot as one of 22 players. That's a large number, of course, and only the 12 best players actually compete in the interscholastic matches; the others compete in what are called "exhibition matches." This didn't faze Maria at all. She had played exhibition matches on the junior varsity team during her freshman and sophomore years, so she understood the process, and her perseverance and determination would eventually pay off.

Maria showed similar grit with her involvement in student government. During her first two years of high school, she served on the Class Council for her grade, and as a junior, she decided to run for the position of secretary. Below is the short speech that she delivered to her classmates prior to the vote:

> When choosing a person to represent your class, as secretary, there are four key things to look for. They include responsibility, leadership, experience, and organization. These four attributes characterize me. I will show responsibility by coming to meetings and show leadership by giving and gathering ideas for events. Another important factor is that I have been on Class Council since 9th grade, and I know what goes on. Last, but certainly not least, I am organized and will keep great notes from the meetings. Please vote for me, Maria LaBate, for secretary, and we will have a great year that includes a spectacular prom and much more.

Unfortunately, Maria didn't win that election, but the loss did not deter her from doing something she truly enjoyed. She continued to serve in student government at the high-school level, and when she went to college, she also found her niche in student government during both her junior and senior years.

2003 — Twelfth Grade

Our summer vacation on Block Island in Rhode Island in July was a phenomenal experience because the girls were old enough (17 and 15) to go out on their own during the day, and the island was small enough that they wouldn't get lost or be in danger. We left our car on the mainland and took the ferry over with our luggage and our bikes, so we could explore the countryside. We biked to two different lighthouses, we went to the beach a few times, we shopped downtown for souvenirs and treats, and we rested and watched movies in the efficiency apartment we rented for the week. The girls also surprised us with an anniversary gift they purchased for us, a framed photograph of the island.

Maria kept a journal during that week, and after one day at the beach, she wrote the following words, words that show her appreciation for small pleasures: "I had fun riding the waves and improving my tan." Later she added, "Then, we went to the store and got some dessert. Dad and Katrina got raspberry slushies, and Mom and I got chocolate-covered raisins, licorice, and raspberry candies to share." That was a great week!

A couple weeks after we returned from Block Island, Maria was baptized. Getting baptized at age 17 may seem somewhat unusual because so many people — including both Barbara and me — were baptized as babies. As mentioned earlier in this text, in the non-denominational Christian church we attended, however, the children are "dedicated" as babies, and, later, they are encouraged to make their own decision about baptism when they are more mature and ready to make that commitment.

In Maria's case, she made that decision prior to her senior year of high school, and she was baptized not in the church but in a nearby lake. Our church encourages the lake baptism because it's more like the baptisms that John the Baptist and Jesus Himself performed in the Bible. Our assistant pastor and youth pastor conducted the services that day, and when Maria's turn came, she walked out into the shallow water near the shore followed by Barbara, Katrina, and me.

We were all in shorts and tee shirts and standing off to the side, in the water above our knees, as the two pastors stood on each side of Maria. Then, our assistant pastor asked Maria a few questions about her desire to be baptized. She consented, and, then, the two pastors each held one of her arms and supported her back as they lowered her into the water, so that she was fully submerged. Maria's baptism symbolized her commitment to Jesus Christ and served as her public declaration in front of other church members and family members. As I also mentioned previously, Maria first committed her life to Christ at the young age of five, and she did it periodically throughout her life, but this event seemed to have so much more meaning to Maria, and we were proud to stand alongside her as she submitted herself to her Creator.

At the end of the summer before Maria's senior year of high school, she reported for tennis practice and by the end of the tryouts, she had earned herself a spot in the top 12 players on the team. In a typical high-school match, those top 12 players compete against other high schools with six girls playing singles matches and six more playing doubles. Maria and a junior named Stephanie played on the third doubles team, and their results helped to influence whether or not the team won the match. That was quite an accomplishment for Maria, and after the final matches of the season, I found myself writing about one match in particular.

The Ironic Beauty of Third Doubles

As the Friday afternoon sun sets on the tennis courts, the bus carrying the opposing football team arrives for its seven-o'clock game. Prior to the kickoff, however, four female tennis players trade serves, groundstrokes, and volleys and try to finish their doubles match before the daylight disappears. Often, these four players, the third doubles teams for both schools, play in a different type of darkness, an obscurity that relegates them to the last court at the last moment. On this particular day, however, their doubles match will determine the final outcome of the overall match between the two teams and may also influence the team seedings for the Sectional Tournament. That combination of obscurity and notoriety is the ironic beauty of third doubles.

Usually, when most people think of tennis, they think of individual singles — and of individual superstars like Roger Federer and Serena Williams. Doubles teams don't get much recognition unless some of the individual stars — like sisters Venus and Serena — team up to play together or unless a famous old-timer comes out of retirement to play the less strenuous and less demanding doubles game. Tennis at the high-school level, however, is really a team game and an extremely democratic game at that.

Typically, the high-school teams play six singles matches and three doubles matches for a total of nine points (smaller schools sometimes play five singles and two doubles). Naturally, the team that wins five of those nine matches wins the team match. Since no player is allowed to play both singles and doubles (again, smaller schools may have different rules), the top 12 players on each team compete, and all nine matches contribute equally to, as sports announcer Jim McKay used to say, "the thrill of victory" or "the agony of defeat." Tennis is so unlike other team sports in that respect.

In most team sports, for instance, certain superstars account for a majority of the scoring. In football, it's the running backs and receivers; in basketball, it's often the center and the shooting guard; and in soccer, hockey, and lacrosse, it's the forwards who spend most of their time in the offensive end. In team tennis, however, the number-one player's match counts for one point, just like the other singles matches and the three doubles matches.

Baseball has a somewhat similar equal-opportunity approach because all nine hitters go to the plate. However, those at the top of the batting order typically get an extra at bat during the course of a game, and those at the bottom of the lineup are often replaced by pinch hitters in difficult situations. Tennis offers no such option; in fact, even if a tennis player is injured during a match, she cannot be replaced. She simply retires, and her point is awarded to the opposition.

The third doubles team is also at the bottom of the order, generally composed of the 11th and 12th best players on the team. At some schools with small rosters, those players may be freshmen or sophomores who are still learning the game. At bigger schools with deeper rosters, though, those spots may be filled by juniors and seniors who have finally earned their way into the starting lineup. The match on this particular day pits seniors Tamar and Katy against Maria and her junior partner, Stephanie. Those same four girls competed earlier in the season, and Maria and Stephanie prevailed 6-4, 6-3, and their team won 6-3. On this particular windy afternoon, though, this third doubles match is the focus of attention, attention that is somewhat unusual for these players at the bottom of the tennis ladder.

The third doubles match generally doesn't attract many fans because most schools have at least nine courts, and all the matches can be played at one time. Under these circumstances, only the relatives and friends of the participants watch third doubles, and even those fans are sometimes distracted and drawn away to watch the more powerful groundstrokes and athleticism displayed in the singles matches, especially the top singles players on each team. If a school has less than nine courts, however, that's when third doubles sometimes draws a crowd.

Since this is an away match for Maria and Stephanie and since the opposing school has only eight courts, the third doubles teams have to wait for one of the first eight matches to finish before their match can commence. Thus, only after one of the singles' matches has been completed can the third-doubles players take the court. Ironically, in this case, they play right next to the number-one singles court.

During their first set, some of the other matches finish, and the team score goes back and forth: The visiting team victory at second singles is followed by home victories in first and second doubles, visiting victories at third and fourth singles, and a home victory at fifth singles. Thus, the team match is tied at 3-3 when Maria and Stephanie win their first set 6-3, and the visitors appear to have the advantage overall. Within minutes, though, the home team wins at first singles, the visitors take sixth singles, and the match is tied at 4-4. At that point, all the attention shifts to the previously ignored third-doubles match.

"Come on, Maria! Come on, Stephanie! You can do it!" shout their teammates as they begin to gather nearby.

"Don't give up, Tamar. Nice shot, Katy," answer the home teammates as they form a small crowd behind the fence near the baseline.

About halfway through the second set, it's apparent to everyone that the momentum has shifted. Tamar and Katy have a 3-1 lead, and if a third set is necessary, the fading light and the oncoming chill will definitely become factors.

As the fifth game of the second set begins, everyone is watching: teammates, coaches, parents, friends, even the bus driver. No one wants to go home, or to the rapidly approaching start of the football game between the same two schools, until this match is decided. Naturally, the tennis at this level is not quite as strong, and the added pressure may produce even more double faults, mis-hits, and unforced errors. Alternatively, the attention of the crowd may spur these weaker players to attempt — and convert — shots they've never even considered before.

Tamar is serving with authority, and Katy is terrorizing the opposition with her net play. Undaunted, Maria and Stephanie persevere. Stephanie chases down groundstrokes in both corners and digs out passing shots to keep one rally alive. Then, Maria finishes the point — and the game — with a swinging backhand volley unlike any shot she's ever executed before on a tennis court.

Each succeeding point is an adventure, and the tension builds gradually. Some points are classic doubles rallies with the baseliners trading crosscourt groundstrokes while those at the net try to sneak across for a volley. Other points are an unpredictable array of shots and movement as players on both teams scurry to keep the ball in play and the point alive. Inevitably, too, after the hotly contested and artistic rallies, the team that won the difficult point often gives it right back with a tentative groundstroke that hits the net or with a too eager volley that sails long.

By the end of game seven, the momentum has shifted again. The visitors' consistency appears to be wearing down the home team, and Maria and Stephanie have crafted a 4-3 lead. Then, just when it looks like they will put the match away, they quickly and easily lose the next game, and a third set seems imminent — yet it never occurs. Frustrated by their lost opportunity and encouraged by their fans, Maria and Stephanie regain their poise and win the next two games to win their doubles match (6-3, 6-4), the team match (5-4), and the number-three seed in the Sectionals. As they calmly walk off the court together, the somewhat stoic victors are hugged and mobbed by their more outgoing and more exuberant teammates.

"Way to go, Maria!"

"Nice job, Stephanie!"

By the following Monday, of course, this third doubles match will be forgotten, and the four participants will return to their tennis obscurity. After all, the teams must begin to prepare for Sectional play, and the top players must get ready for the Individual Sectional Tournament. For one glorious, fall afternoon, however, Tamar and Katy and Maria and Stephanie came together for their final regular season match, and at that moment of autumnal color and fading light, all eyes were upon them. Surprisingly, their third doubles match provided exceptional beauty and thrilling drama for all who were fortunate enough to attend.

One other highlight of Maria's senior year was the opportunity she had to teach elementary students on a limited basis. During that academic year, she took a course in Early Childhood Education, and to no one's surprise, she earned an "A." The best part of the course from Maria's perspective, though, was that for three months in the spring, she was allowed to leave the high school to visit and teach periodically in one of the district's grade schools. Granted, she only accumulated a limited number of hours per month, but we could see her enthusiasm when she spoke about her young students, and the overall experience reinforced her desire to be a teacher.

Also, during the Easter break of Maria's senior year, she went on a third missions' trip. This trip to Belize in Central America was sponsored solely by our church, and each volunteer had to raise about $1,000 by asking for donations from family members and church members and also by doing work in the community such as babysitting, raking leaves, and cleaning homes. Maria was one of the older students on this trip, and she was again blessed to share the experience with Katrina.

During their time in Belize, the team lived in a dormitory hosted by a missionary couple from Long Island who had lived in that area for five years. During the daytime hours, the team helped to build a small home for a middle-aged woman who had never owned a place of her own. They also participated in an evening vacation Bible school by teaching Bible stories, leading craft activities, and performing songs and skits for the young people in the community.

The evening activities were so much more fun for Maria who hoped to be a teacher, and she especially enjoyed the interaction with the local young people. In her journal from that week, Maria admitted that spreading cement was "HARD WORK," but she really enjoyed interacting with her students, and she wrote that "It was exciting to be able to use my Spanish." She even volunteered to share her life story with everyone at a church service, a story that was translated, so everyone could understand.

Before I finish describing Maria's high-school years, I feel like I should write a few words about her relationships with the young men in her life. Maria never seriously dated anyone during her time in high school. Yes, she had young men who were interested in her, and, yes, she was definitely interested in some of her classmates. However, the perfect combination between the two never quite lined up. The male students who liked her didn't appeal to her, and the ones who did appeal to her either already had girlfriends or simply had their eyes on someone else. Maria, like many young ladies in her circumstances, definitely struggled with this dilemma because she wanted to be her normal sweet self to everyone, but she didn't want to falsely encourage her admirers, and, by contrast, she was usually disappointed when those she admired were sometimes cold to her for the same reason. As a result, Maria often attended the formal dances at school with other girls who did not actually have a date, or she sometimes attended with a male friend who found himself in a similar circumstance. Bottom line: Maria's experience in this area was likely very similar to what many young people, both male and female, experience during their formative years.

2004 — Freshman Year in College

The year 2004 was a time of mixed experiences for Maria. During the first half of the year, she completed her final year of high school, and during the second half, she left home for her first semester away at college. One experience was positive; one was not.

Like most high-school seniors, Maria looked forward to those traditional milestone events: college visitations, the senior ball, end-of-year award ceremonies, and graduation.

In her college search, Maria visited five schools: three state schools and two private schools, only one of which was nearby. I remember one visit in particular because during the big, morning presentations in the gym for both students and parents, Maria was not impressed, and she indicated that to me. After lunch, however, she toured the campus in a much smaller student group with a female student guide, and the two of them conversed quickly and easily. By the end of the tour, Maria had changed her mind and decided she wanted to attend that school, a Christian school in Pennsylvania, which was a five-hour drive from our home. The decision was so typical for Maria — negativity at first based on a cold, bureaucratic initial impression but positivity once she made that personal connection with another student.

With that college decision behind her, Maria enjoyed her Senior Ball with a good friend from church, she was fortunate to win an education award at the academic assembly, and she posed for plenty of pictures with her friends at their outdoor graduation ceremony.

I remember that graduation time vividly because I knew it marked a major milestone in Maria's life. When she was born, I recall thinking that we would enjoy her for the next 18 years or so before she moved on to the next stage of her life. Not that we wouldn't still be involved but that she would be so much more independent. In other words, I was grateful for that first major stage of her life, and I was so proud of her as she prepared for the next stage. I was thinking about all this as we hosted Maria's graduation party on the Fourth of July, about two weeks after the actual graduation ceremony.

On the day of the party, we had one tent set up on the back deck and one on part of the lawn on the side of our house. We also borrowed a volleyball and a net and marked out the boundaries on the other part of that lawn, and we even moved our ping-pong table from the basement out to the driveway. We were all set to host family members, neighbors, friends, and, of course, Maria's classmates. Before we ate, though, I wanted to say a prayer over the food and to give thanks for this beautiful girl who we were celebrating on that day. I managed to thank God for the food, but before I said a word about what a special girl Maria was, I broke down. I couldn't get another word out without bawling completely, so I simply closed my eyes, bowed my head, and shook it from side to side before Barbara bailed me out by saying a loud "Amen."

Thinking about that moment later, I recalled again the poem I mentioned earlier, a poem written by American author Edgar Lee Masters in 1916, a poem entitled "Silence." In that poem, Masters explains that some emotions or experiences cannot be expressed verbally at the time, so we hold on to those moments, we reflect upon them, and, when we are ready, we write about them. One of his examples was evident in this case: "the silence of a great love" (line 34). This book, of course, is a love letter of sorts for her, my extended reflection on Maria's life and the emotions and experiences we shared.

Maria spent the remainder of the summer working at both the bakery and as the hostess at a local restaurant, and by preparing to furnish her dormitory room. Unfortunately, the transition from home living to campus living was not as smooth as we all had hoped.

Since Maria had played tennis in high school, we brought her to campus a week early to try out for the team, and she earned a spot on the squad. She wasn't yet strong enough as a player to compete in the matches against other colleges, and she also struggled with ankle problems, but overall, she was happy to be part of the team. Unfortunately, her happiness began to deteriorate when her two roommates arrived, and Maria also began her part-time, on-campus job, a job that was a mandatory part of her financial-aid package.

The roommate situation was problematic because the school needed to squeeze three girls into a room intended for two — tight quarters indeed. In addition, Maria's job required her to clean the bathrooms in the dormitory where she lived. As a result, since Maria was often at tennis practice or working, her two roommates bonded without her, and they, and others, often treated Maria as if she were Cinderella, the cleaning girl at their service.

When Barbara and I called Maria or visited the campus to watch her play tennis, we could tell she was struggling to balance her school work, her cleaning job, and her tennis. In fact, she wrote about her coping mechanisms in an essay for her first-year seminar class: "When I talk with my mom on the phone, she encourages me to keep believing in God, and at times, it is her voice that encourages me to go to church when I do not feel like it."

Maria also wrote about her new friend. "I have a prayer partner here at college . . . We also share inspiring verses with one another, encourage one another, and care for each other." As a result of that friendship, Maria was already planning to room with that girl in the spring, so we all felt optimistic about Maria's return to campus after the Christmas break. Little did we know that the early part of 2005 would be even more of a struggle for her.

In the midst of that difficult first semester, though, we also saw maturity and growth. In late September, we drove down to watch Maria play tennis, and when the coach asked someone to pray before the match, Maria boldly volunteered. Then, during her exhibition match that day, Maria noticed that her opponent was struggling physically, so Maria offered that girl the Pop-Tart that Maria had brought for herself. And during the entire weekend, Maria included Katrina in all the activities, so Katrina could get a feel for college life on campus, and she even encouraged Katrina to attend the same school if the school offered a program that she desired. What a great older sister!

2005 — Sophomore Year in College

During the long Christmas vacation, Maria visited the home of her new roommate/prayer partner and felt positive about the upcoming spring semester. As her parents, Barbara and I were feeling good too because she had apparently put that difficult first semester behind her, a semester in which she had, to her credit, achieved good grades and earned her spot on the tennis team.

Unfortunately, those positives did not outweigh the Cinderella experience that still haunted her. During her first week of classes in late January, Maria slipped into a mild depression, and a counselor on campus called to say he didn't think she could endure the next four months under those circumstances. Maria agreed. As her dad, I again wanted Maria to push through it all and persevere, but when Barbara asked that counselor what he would do if Maria were his daughter, he said he would bring her home. So, wanting to avoid the mistake we made when we asked Maria to persevere with that difficult fifth-grade teacher, we did not ask her to push through again, and we allowed her to withdraw from classes. The next day, Barbara and I drove five hours to her campus, packed up all of her possessions, and brought her home.

Maria's first few months at home were a struggle for all of us because she had nothing to do — no schoolwork and no job. She kept a journal during that time, and she admitted the following: "I want to appear as if I have things under control at all times when I do not. No one can have it all together. God is the missing piece in everyone's hurting life. Also, over these last 18 years, I feel as if I've lost my heart."

When we found her journal from this time period after she passed, we were shocked to read that she had also written about suicide: "At times, I have thought about suicide but would never actually do it. When I felt that I was real down in the dumps, I would either go to church youth group or be with my friends. I believe in the power of thinking positively."

Fortunately, the safe and comfortable environment at home and a few sessions with a nearby counselor helped Maria to gradually reunite with old friends and, later, to seek a job, ideally one in the education field where she eventually hoped to pursue a career. By April, Maria was helping out at a nearby, family-run day care, and the family members working there also helped her and encouraged her.

With all that support, Maria began to assert more of her own individuality. She made new friends. She began to attend a church different from the one where she grew up. And she found a part-time job in a coffee shop that had just opened, an environment that suited her well and where she also trained to become a barista. She loved working there. Finally, in July, almost the entire extended family (about 20 of us) on Barbara's side traveled to the Outer Banks of North Carolina for a week together in a big, rented home near the Atlantic Ocean. We played lots of tennis together, and we spent lots of time in the pool out back and at the nearby ocean beach. Maria even managed to meet up with two of her college friends.

Maria also began taking evening summer classes at the community college where I worked, and she later decided to complete her second year there. She even played a significant role on the school's tennis team:

competing and earning victories (in actual matches, not exhibition matches) in both singles and doubles.

During Maria's first week of the fall semester, though, she was still a bit hesitant and tentative. When she had time between classes, she retreated to The Writing Center in the Library where I worked. There, while I helped students with their essays and research papers, she sat quietly and did her own reading and homework. Only after she became comfortable with her classmates and tennis teammates did she begin to socialize in the Campus Center or in the open areas on campus. As her dad, of course, I enjoyed seeing her often and watching her work in my domain, but I knew it was much better for her to be out there on her own again, regaining her confidence and establishing personal relationships. Thus, 2005 ended on an upbeat note for Maria and helped her return to her original plan of earning a four-year degree in education in order to become an elementary-school teacher.

2006 — Junior Year in College

The year 2006 was a good one all around for Maria. She completed her second semester at the community college in the spring, and she returned to the Christian college in the fall, and both experiences were positive.

Though Maria did not earn a diploma from that community college, she did complete a full schedule of classes again in the spring, and she became so much more involved with friends, both old and new. Yes, she was still living at home during the spring, but she was out and about often in the surrounding communities, so much so that we bought her a GPS device to help her find her way around. Like many in her generation, Maria did not often consult maps when she drove to be with her friends or to attend various activities or concerts in the area. Somehow, she always found her way to the event; she just couldn't find her way home. Then, she'd call me late at night, she'd tell me where she was, and I would consult my local atlas and stay on the phone with her until we got her back to a highway she recognized. Before we got her the GPS, she joked that she would just use 1-800-CALL-DAD to find her way home. At times, her driving adventures were fun and lighthearted, but at other times, her late phone calls woke me up, and I worried a bit when she found herself out in the countryside or in less than desirable surroundings. Thank God for His protection over her — and for the new technology.

    Once Maria was officially readmitted to the Christian college she had attended previously, she began to reconnect with some friends there, and she planned a much better situation for herself. She arranged to room with another young lady in a completely different dormitory on the other side of campus. This new situation allowed her to escape the reminders of her Cinderella experience, and her new working experience as a barista also permitted her to find a similar job off campus, so she wouldn't need the on-campus cleaning position. Fortunately, too, she intended to compete on the tennis team, and, as she had done in high school, she hoped to be part of the student government. Our Maria was excited to return to the full campus experience, and we could not have been happier. All of us.

Just as we had done during Maria's first semester away, Barbara, Katrina, and I traveled with Maria to Pennsylvania to help her transport all her stuff and help her set up her room. Ironically, through poor planning on our part, we arrived on campus with just enough time for Maria to don her tennis gear and hustle off to the courts for her first two-hour practice. As a result, Katrina and I had to do all the heavy lifting and carrying to Maria's third-floor room without the benefit of an elevator (a complicated story you don't want to hear), and Barbara unpacked and organized everything. Of course, we teased Maria about that experience, but she didn't care; she felt like she was back where she needed to be, and the semester went so well for her.

She and her new roommate got along well and participated in lots of activities together. Maria earned good grades in all of her classes. She enjoyed tennis again (though she hadn't earned a competitive position). Her barista job was fun for her, and she finally found a position in student government as part of the Peer Review Board (a student organization that hears cases and determines punishment for violations of student rules).

During the spring, Maria also acted in a play called *Las Paredes (The Walls)* as part of her Spanish course. The entire production was in Spanish, so even though Barbara and I knew we would struggle to understand what was going on, we eagerly made the five-hour trip to see Maria perform and take pictures of her and her castmates afterwards. We were so proud of Maria and her recovery. When we brought her home about 18 months earlier, we weren't sure that she'd ever make it back, but she did. Way to go, Girl!

2007 — Senior Year in College

The spring of Maria's junior year seemed pretty normal compared to the ups and downs of her first five semesters of college. She had comfortably settled back into campus life with a roommate she liked, a curriculum she loved, a role in student government she appreciated, and a part-time job she enjoyed. She even found a church off campus that she liked. And when she came home periodically for a weekend, she brought a college friend with her, and she still helped out with the youth group at her new church.

During the summer before her senior year, Maria spent most of her time working as a counselor at an overnight Christian camp for young children. Though the camp was only 45 minutes from our home, she slept in the dormitory and supervised a small group of middle-school girls who were learning to ride horses and take care of them. Maria's primary daytime task was to help out with the volleyball classes and also help coordinate other activities when necessary. The job was good preparation for her teaching career because she also had to prepare regular Bible studies for her campers and help them get along with one another.

The beginning of Maria's senior year of college turned out to be more busy than she would have liked. She returned to campus early to play tennis again, and not only did she earn a spot in the regular lineup as part of the third doubles team, but she and her partner also won their first match. Unfortunately, after that first success, Maria decided she had to quit the team because in addition to her regular schedule of classes, she also had to make time to observe a teacher in an actual school and prepare to serve as a student teacher herself in the spring. I think she felt she couldn't do justice to both tennis and her education requirements, so to my dismay, she gave up tennis. Yes, I know she made the right decision, and I was proud of her for it, but I did so enjoy watching her compete on a college level. My loss.

Maria also had a unique living arrangement during that time. She had somehow arranged to live with five other senior girls in a house near the edge of the campus. The house was actually owned and maintained by the college and was simply another option for campus housing just like the dormitories. I honestly don't recall how she ended up there or what she had to do to qualify to live there, but I do remember that she was excited about it because some of the other girls were also education majors and friends.

Regarding that observation requirement, Maria kept a journal of a kindergarten class to which she was assigned, and while most of her journal entries from that experience focused on what the children were learning and doing, one key entry explains Maria's desire to teach: "I love kids. I love to see them learn."

2008 — Final Semester in College

During Maria's final year on campus, she also served as the Chairperson of the Peer Review Board; as mentioned earlier, she had been a committee member during the previous academic year. As the Chairperson, she, along with a college staff member, supervised a small committee of students whose job was to discipline student rulebreakers and restore those individuals back to the college community. In an article that Maria wrote that year for the student newspaper, she explained, "When students who have violated college standards come before us, the Board's job is to determine whether students are responsible for the alleged violation and, if so, to determine sanctions that are appropriate, just, and redemptive."

Maria so enjoyed that particular task, and she talked to us often about her responsibilities in that position. As a reward for her commitment to her fellow students, Maria and her committee members enjoyed two special events: sitting in the audience as Democratic Presidential Candidates Barack Obama and Hillary Clinton visited her school for a televised "Compassion Forum" prior to the 2008 Pennsylvania Presidential Primary, and later in the spring, she was invited with other students to be part of a dinner gathering with the college president in her home on campus.

Maria also took two education courses during her final semester on campus, but her most significant task was her student-teaching experience, a 12-week adventure that began in mid-February and continued through the first week of May. She was assigned to work as a fourth-grade teacher at a school that was about 30 minutes from her campus. The class consisted of 16 boys and 11 girls, and Maria's supervising teacher was phenomenal. She was upbeat and encouraging, and she helped Maria overcome her initial struggles: nervousness, failure to engage all the students, and difficulty managing time during her lessons.

One of Maria's first lessons was on the history of Valentine's Day, and throughout the late winter and spring, she had the chance to also teach all of the following: math (multiplication and division, and measuring area and perimeter); history (William Penn, Betsy Ross, and Ben Franklin); science (weather, the planets, and the greenhouse effect); geography (the United States and Canada); and, my favorite, writing (spelling, punctuation, similes, and persuasive essays).

Naturally, Maria's supervising teacher gave her constructive criticism on a daily basis, and her college supervisor observed her weekly, and in his final report, he wrote the following: "I have seen tremendous growth in Maria during this semester. She has grown in confidence and control of the classroom. She has good rapport with students and staff. Her quiet style has been most effective. She is at ease in the teaching situation. Planning, preparation, and presentations are well done. She makes the necessary effort to succeed.

Miss LaBate is an enthusiastic and dependable young lady. She would be a welcome addition to any staff."

In addition to that final evaluation of Maria's teaching competence, that same gentleman made the following statement to Maria in one of his earlier weekly reports, a statement that makes me, as her dad, especially proud: "Even the secretary tells me how friendly you are."

Finally, at the end of Maria's 12 weeks, her students bombarded her with cards, drawings, letters of appreciation, and thank-you notes. An excerpt from one of her male students stands out: "I've enjoyed getting to know you. You are one of the best teachers I've had. Thank you for teaching me how to do division. I used to hate it, but now I love it, thanks to you. Thank you for being there when I needed help. I'll never forget you."

As a parting gift to Maria, her supervising teacher gave Maria a copy of the book *Chicken Soup for the Teacher's Soul*, a book her teacher inscribed in this way: "I truly have enjoyed watching you throughout your student-teacher experience. This journey that you and I walked through together is special to me. The children you teach will be the lucky ones!"

Maria graduated from college on Saturday morning May 17, 2008. Considering what she had been through during her freshman year, the fact that she still graduated on schedule in four years is amazing, perhaps one of her greatest accomplishments. Naturally, Barbara, Katrina, and I traveled to campus to be there for the special activities the night before and the graduation ceremony itself. My parents and one of my sisters also attended the ceremony and went out for a meal with us afterwards. Later that evening, I'm sure Maria would have liked to simply relax and enjoy her accomplishment, but she still had one more task to fulfill before she could actually receive her diploma.

In order to officially graduate, Maria had to complete her final three credits, which involved a three-week trip to Spain, and she and the rest of the group had to fly out the following Monday. Obviously, she couldn't relax. She had to pack for that trip plus we had to get all the rest of her stuff out of her place and bring it home. Maria was stressing big time, and she didn't think she could go through with the trip. Yes, we could all empathize with her exhaustion, but we couldn't let her blow off the course just because she was tired. So as much as we could, Barbara, Katrina, and I took turns encouraging her and helping her get ready, and by Sunday morning, as scheduled, we were on our way home, and Maria was on a bus to New York City for her flight to Spain on Monday. I have a feeling she slept the entire way.

As part of that final course in Spain, Maria was required to keep a journal, and she had to write some portions of it in Spanish, a language that she loved. Her group landed in Madrid, then took another flight to Sevilla where she lived with a family for about ten days. Later, they spent a few days in Nerja and Granada before returning to Madrid for a flight home. During that time, she visited cathedrals and museums, and she seemed especially mesmerized by demonstrations of flamenco dancers, guitar makers, and matadors. On the final page of her journal, she used Spanglish to describe her adventure as an "eventful, amazing viaje (trip)." And her written

Spanish was pretty good, too, as evidenced by only minor corrections in red ink from her teacher, and a final grade of 91. Way to go, Maria. When I read that journal a few years after Maria passed, I used it to write a blogpost which I have included here.

My Recent Trip to Spain

During my final year of work in 2020, as I planned for retirement, I imagined that Barbara and I would do some traveling. A few years earlier, for instance, we had the opportunity to travel to Italy, Greece, and Turkey on a 13-day cruise that we thoroughly enjoyed. Thus, I began to think about other countries I'd like to visit. I thought about Israel because I would like to walk where Jesus walked, and I thought about Ireland because having already explored the Italian half of my heritage, I also want to explore the Irish half. Unfortunately, the COVID 19 situation and quarantine effectively postponed all those thoughts and adventures for a time. Fortunately, I was able to visit Spain during that time for three weeks with my daughter Maria.

"But that's impossible," you're thinking. And you're absolutely right. There's no way I was able to travel to Spain under those circumstances. And if you know me or if you've read some of my previous posts, you know that our daughter Maria passed away in 2016 at age 30 after a short battle with cancer. However, I was able to vicariously travel to Spain with Maria because she went there in 2008 when she was a senior in college, and she left behind the journal she kept during that unique experience. I used that journal to help me describe her journey.

Before I begin, though, you may wonder why I waited so long to read that journal. Honestly, I think I was overwhelmed by everything that Maria had left behind. Let's face the truth; no one expects a 30-year-old to die, so when it happens, life slows down, and the number of tasks accumulates. We had to empty out her apartment and deal with all of her furniture, her clothes, and her possessions while also dealing with the emptiness in our hearts and in our family gatherings. The journey is long and painful. On top of that, Maria kept quite a few journals during her lifetime, so as we sorted through her belongings, we set all of those journals aside, along with all of her photographs, with the idea that at some point, we would go through them. That time has come.

As a writer myself, I feel I should also explain that Maria and I share one common quality regarding our writing: inconsistency. We don't write every single day. Instead, we write sporadically as time permits, or we write during certain periods of life that are special or unique. This three-week overseas trip for Maria was obviously a once-in-a-lifetime experience, but the trip and the accompanying journal were also requirements for school, tasks that she needed to complete if she wanted to graduate. In addition, she needed to write at least half of her journal in Spanish. So, if you were to browse through the pages of that journal, you would see not only the blue and black ink of Maria's pens but also the red ink of her professor who would periodically read the journal and point out Maria's incorrect verb tenses or Spanish vocabulary while also commenting on Maria's observations about Spanish culture. Are you ready for takeoff? Let's go.

Maria and her fellow adventurers flew out of JFK Airport in New York City on Monday, May 19, 2008, two days after her graduation. This three-credit experience would serve as their final academic task prior to receiving their diplomas. After a six-hour flight to Madrid, the students and leaders switched planes and flew for an additional hour to the town of Sevilla, which is in southern Spain, about 120 miles north of Gibraltar and the Alboran Sea which separates Spain from Morocco. After their plane touched down in Sevilla, the tour guides met the students and escorted them to a hotel where they ate lunch and took a nap. On that first day, Maria recorded the food she ate (a veggie wrap with chicken and French fries for lunch with a vegetable lasagna for dinner) and her activities: a guided tour of the city during the afternoon and an informal walk with friends through Sevilla that night. Having grown up in a quiet suburban town in upstate New York, Maria seemed fascinated by the fact that an "evening in Spain doesn't start until 8:00 p.m."

The next day, Maria and her classmates left the hotel and moved in with local host families for a 10-day stay in Sevilla, a city of 700,000 (roughly the same population as Washington, D.C., or Boston). Maria lived with three other American girls in this Spanish home, and she loved it. In fact, near the end of her stay with the family, she had to write an essay about the benefits of studying abroad, and Maria highlighted the following: "You can try new food, you can practice or learn a new language. While adjusting to a new culture and stepping out of your comfort zone can be difficult, it is well worth it." Later, near the end of her stay there, she added: "I enjoyed living with my host mom and getting to know the city. It is so great how families just let you stay with them."

During their time in Sevilla, the students had daily classes which were a combination of actual classes about Spain, its history and culture, along with tours of various locations. For example, they visited The Cathedral of Saint Mary, one of the largest churches in the world, and they visited the Museum of Fine Arts which has paintings from the medieval period to the early 20th century.

On one particular day, the group made a day trip to Córdoba, which is about 90 miles northeast of Sevilla. There, Maria saw the ruins of a Roman bridge over the Guadalquivir River; she saw the Great Mosque of Córdoba, a mosque so big that a Christian church was later built inside the mosque; and she visited an old, Jewish neighborhood, a visit that prompted her to write, "It's neat how they (the Jews) were able to coexist with the Muslims and Christians and share ideas."

The students also enjoyed Spanish culture firsthand. One experience was a day at the bullfights, and, quite honestly, I was surprised that Maria didn't write anything about the bullfights. Instead, she was much more impressed by a later visit to a workshop where a craftsman made guitars and by a demonstration of flamenco dancing with singers and guitarists. She described the dancing as "fantastica." She was especially intrigued by the storytelling aspect of the dance. She was so intrigued, in fact, that in her journal, she wrote that she enjoyed the paintings of Joaquín Sorolla y Bastida because he often used bright colors to demonstrate this dancing aspect of the culture. Overall, Maria thoroughly enjoyed her time in

Sevilla, and she especially enjoyed her time with her host family. To remember that portion of her trip, she purchased a tote bag with the name "Sevilla" inscribed on the side.

During the next portion of the tour, Maria's group traveled southeast and spent four nights (Thursday through Sunday) in Nerja, which is part of the Costa del Sol (Coast of the Sun) near the Mediterranean Sea, about 160 miles from Sevilla. They slept in a hostel, and their long weekend in this area was less active and much more relaxed than their previous stay in Sevilla. Yes, they toured a nearby cathedral, but they also spent parts of Friday, Saturday, and Sunday at the beach. Our fair-skinned Maria didn't go into the water each day, but she enjoyed resting on the sand with her friends, experiencing new things, and making observations.

One day, for instance, she tasted yucca for the first time at lunch, and she described it as a "potato" or "thicker French fries." She also seemed mildly surprised that some bathers did not wear swimsuits. Finally, she mentioned that on one of her walks to the beach, she and her friend got lost, but a local woman helped them. Writing about that experience later and also about a shopping trip one night, Maria noted that the people near the water seemed more friendly and more helpful than the people farther away from the coast.

Their next destination was Granada, which is back inland to the northeast, and, again, they stayed in a hostel. Unfortunately, Maria wasn't feeling well that first day because she had become dehydrated. By evening, though, she felt better, and they toured the city and went to a spot where they had a beautiful view of the Alhambra, which was originally constructed as a fortress and later converted to a royal palace. In her journal, Maria seemed fascinated by the gypsies who lived in the area in "simple, small caves" and were "very often flamenco dancers."

On another day, they visited the house of Ana and learned how to make tortillas Españoles, which Maria described as "delicious." Ana also taught them how to clap as a way to accompany the different rhythms of Spanish dances. Maria really enjoyed watching Ana dance and experiencing the emotions of the dance's story.

On Thursday, June 5, the group rose at 5:00 a.m., in order to catch a 6:40 train from Granada to Madrid. When they arrived, they had lunch, and Maria enjoyed "arroz con leche" (rice with milk, or rice pudding), which she described as "very typical" for Spain and "very good."

After lunch, they walked around and saw the Plaza de Espana, a statue of Don Quixote and Sancho Panza, and the Palacio Real (Royal Palace), which used to be the King's residence but is now used for office workers. Maria thought the building was "beautiful" and was hoping to tour the inside, but it was closed when they were there.

On Friday, June 6, they visited the Prado, Spain's national art museum, and Maria saw works by Diego Velázquez and Francisco Goya among others. After lunch, Maria returned to the Palacio Real, again hoping to get inside, but something official was happening, so she couldn't. She was "muy triste" (very sad). At that point, she decided to walk to the subway to go back to the hotel, but she got lost. Fortunately, this gave her an opportunity to use her Spanish to ask for directions.

Later that evening, she went to the theater to see *La Bella y La Bestia* (*Beauty and the Beast*) which she thoroughly enjoyed.

At the end of her journal, Maria wrote: "It was a good ending to an eventful, amazing viaje (trip) and learning experience."

Then, she also wrote a final note to her teacher. "Thank you for everything. MUCHAS GRACIAS."

In response, her teacher wrote in red ink: "Gracias tambien por tus contribuciones a la experiencia!" ("Thank you also for your contributions to the experience.") As mentioned earlier, her teacher also gave her a final grade of 91 on the journal project.

As I was reading this journal, I began to really appreciate the fact that Maria recorded so many of her experiences and her thoughts in this volume and others. I also found myself wanting to know more about the cities and the specific landmarks she toured. Consequently, I have added Spain to the list of countries I want to visit. Yes, I want to walk where Maria walked.

2009

The years after Maria's 2008 graduation from college were a bit hectic for her because she was unable to find a full-time teaching job and was living at home with us. As a result, she was working part-time jobs, such as her new position at Dunkin Donuts, and other temporary jobs until she could find more secure employment. During those early post-college days, Maria also served as a substitute teacher in numerous school districts, getting called sporadically and only for one day at a time, never a long-term assignment. In addition, Maria worked as a group leader for an after-school program at the same elementary school she attended for grades two through five. In that position, she supervised the children and led them in crafts, outside play, and games in the gymnasium until their working parents arrived. I couldn't help but admire Maria's willingness to keep working with young people as much as she could in her quest to find a full-time teaching job.

Fortunately, almost a full year after her graduation, she was finally able to secure a long-term substitute assignment in one school district where she served as a math specialist for roughly four months. In that position, she and another instructor worked one-on-one with grade-school students who were struggling with math, and Maria and the other instructor tried to bring those students up to speed. Though the assignment wasn't exactly the situation she wanted — she really wanted her own fourth-grade class of students — it did give her a normal work schedule for a time and allowed her to save some money, so she could eventually move out on her own.

During that time, too, Maria participated in a fellowship group sponsored by our church, a group made up of college students and other young people who were just beginning their careers. They usually met weekly to study the Bible and other Christian literature as they tried to figure out what God's Word meant to them and what plans He had for their lives. Through that group, Maria met quite a few others who, like her, took their faith seriously and tried to spread the "Good News" of Jesus Christ. In fact, they would sometimes go to a nearby city and stand on street corners and try to engage passersby in conversations about the Bible, something I would never do even as a grown man. They also participated in charitable activities like passing out socks, blankets, and food to the homeless and volunteering at a nearby shelter: serving meals to the residents or working in the used-clothing store sponsored by the shelter. In fact, during successive Thanksgiving feasts, Maria encouraged Barbara, Katrina, and me to help prepare and serve the meal for the homeless one year, and together, Maria and I delivered meals to the private homes of elderly residents the next.

Subsequently, Maria began to attend a different church in our area. Looking back at that time period, I think she was trying to establish herself and strengthen her faith by doing so. In that new church, she was no longer "Jim and Barbara's older daughter." Instead, she was free to be herself, and she thrived by volunteering to teach Sunday School classes to the young children, an activity that she loved and one that she could add to her resume as she continued to search for a full-time teaching job. Naturally, too, she met even more people her age in that church, and they socialized often by meeting in one another's homes or by sharing meals at restaurants. So despite her inability to find her ideal teaching job, Maria was making the best of her situation and moving forward. As her dad, I was proud of her and curious to see what she would do next.

2010

During the spring of 2010, Maria decided to be a bit more proactive in her job search. Traditionally, the best way to find a full-time teaching job is to serve as a substitute teacher for a year or two in various school districts. The rationale is that substitute teaching would not only give the new teachers needed experience in the classroom, but it would also allow them to learn about upcoming retirements in the school districts and, thus, job openings. That experience would also allow these young people to get to know the principals who might want to hire them.

In Maria's case, she had subbed for almost two full years in numerous local school districts, but few openings existed because the economy was still pretty bad during that era (due to the mortgage crisis and the 2007-2009 recession). As a result, older teachers were holding on to their jobs longer than they might have originally, and aspiring teachers had to do whatever they could to survive. In fact, one night when our family went out to eat, our waiter mentioned that he had been subbing for almost five years, and he hadn't yet secured a full-time position. That particular story may have caused Maria to rethink her job-search strategy.

As a result of substitute teaching in numerous school districts, Maria had previously met quite a few other teachers who were in a similar position. Some of them had mentioned to her that North Carolina had a teacher shortage at that time and was hiring quite a few teachers from the northern states. When Maria asked about the process, they mentioned job fairs that occurred in the spring and were designed to find and hire teachers for the following fall. When Maria explored the possibility, she heard about a job fair in Pinehurst, North Carolina, and since Barbara and Katrina were unable to travel that weekend, Maria asked me if I'd want to go with her. "I'd love to go," I answered immediately. "Sign me up." Mind you, I wasn't going to look for a new job myself, but I just wanted to spend time with her and perhaps help her navigate what would undoubtedly be a major move.

We flew into Durham and rented a car on a Thursday, so Maria would be fresh and ready to go bright and early on Friday morning. The fair was held at the Pinehurst Resort Golf Course, and after filling out some paperwork, Maria had interviews with representatives from three different school districts. Then, she enjoyed lunch with some of the other future teachers before we drove off to visit a couple of the nearby schools.

One school, I have to admit, looked ideal. It was a nearby private school, and the person she spoke to was friendly and encouraging. The other school we saw that day was out in the country a bit and deserted by the time we got there. This second school was not at all appealing; it looked run down, and the setting was not inviting. As Maria's dad, I would not have wanted to leave her alone in that environment so far from home.

Then, after the school visits, we also toured a nearby apartment complex which was attractive and reminded me of the complex where we lived when Maria was born and again later before we bought our first home. By the end of the day, we were both exhausted, but optimistic, and we flew home the next morning.

Unfortunately for Maria, the trip did not produce any positive results: no second interviews, no follow-up phone calls, and not even a thank-you card from any of the people who interviewed her. She was disappointed, of course, but when she shared her disappointment with her friends, I heard her say that it was simply "not God's will at this time." What a mature reaction from a classy young lady.

Personally, I had mixed emotions. On one hand, I wanted to see Maria succeed and achieve her dreams, but, honestly, I wanted her to achieve those dreams nearby — not a plane ride or a 14-hour trip in the car. I didn't tell her, of course, any of that until well after we had returned home. By then, she had overcome her disappointment, so she laughed heartily when I explained to her that the telephone number 1-800-CALL-DAD did not take calls from out of state.

Next, during that summer, Maria worked for a private company scoring standardized tests of third and fourth graders in both math and English language arts. I think the scoring work itself was somewhat boring, but Maria seemed to really enjoy her co-workers because they were mostly teachers. Some, like

Maria, were young and looking for a full-time job, and some were retired teachers who were scoring tests just to keep themselves busy. During lunch hour each day and during breaks, Maria heard about job opportunities from some of the younger folks, and she listened to stories from the older teachers who were eager to share classroom experiences from their careers.

In the fall, Maria continued to juggle her substitute teaching with her job at Dunkin Donuts with an additional weekend position at the same country store/bakery where she worked in high school. It's no wonder she sometimes felt as if she were moving backward instead of forward. She even tried working with Barbara in a network marketing business, selling memberships to buy safer products for the home. And to Maria's credit, in the midst of that crazy work schedule and with tight finances, she did manage to move out on her own. She rented a room in a house with two other friends about 20 minutes south of our home, and she was so excited to move her furniture in there and begin to decorate her bedroom walls. I specifically remember shopping with her to buy a mirror for the back of her bedroom door and an inspirational decoration with butterflies that she hung on the wall over her bed, a decoration that we still possess and one that hangs near the staircase in our home today. It reads as follows:

> Live, Love, Laugh
> Dance as though no one is watching.
> Love as though you have never loved before.
> Sing as though no one can hear you.
> Live as though heaven is on earth.

2011

By the spring of 2011, Maria still hadn't found her ideal job, but she did find an opportunity that appealed to her desire to have her own classroom and her own students. A nearby daycare center needed a certified teacher for the three- and four-year old students. Maria interviewed for the job and accepted the position. She was excited and eager to begin, not only because she would finally be in charge day by day (Monday, Wednesday, and Friday for the four-year-old children and Tuesday and Thursday for the three-year-old children), but she would also be working with people she knew; one assistant teacher was an old family friend who had taught at the nursery-school level for many years, and the other was a few years younger than Maria, a girl who grew up in our neighborhood and was just entering the education field herself. Together, these three would instruct and supervise the children each day while the day care owner/director served as their supervisor and handled all the business details.

Maria was definitely in her element, in charge and excited to be teaching young people. In fact, I had the opportunity to observe her one day. As I recall, the owner and the older assistant were both unavailable that day, and I was free, so Maria got permission for me to be present just in case any problems occurred. Fortunately, nothing out of the ordinary happened, and I was free to merely observe my Maria as she welcomed the students, read stories to them, practiced their numbers and colors with them, handled one-on-one issues, and supervised them in the classroom and on the playground out back. I have to admit, that day was one of my best days ever in a classroom.

Unfortunately, by December, Maria realized that particular position was not for her. When she wrote her official resignation letter to the daycare owner early in the month, Maria explained her reasoning:

> Thank you for the opportunity to work here, but I need to give my notice. I've enjoyed working alongside all of you. I've loved being able to teach and interact with the kids. It's been a great experience to have my own classroom. I'm giving my notice because I've come to the realization that daycare is not for me. I desire to teach older children. In addition, I am experiencing some temporary health problems. I am dealing with intense back and ankle pain which is preventing me from performing my job" (health issues that had always bothered Maria during her years of playing tennis).

In addition, Maria also wrote a letter directly to the parents:

> Your children are dear to my heart. I have enjoyed getting to know each and every one of you along with your children. We have experienced some wonderful moments together including the Easter performance, a wonderful summer program, field trips to the swimming pool, apple picking, and so many other events. I have loved seeing your children become good learners, excellent listeners, and good friends throughout my time here. Unfortunately, I will be leaving at the end of December. I love each and every one of your children, but I desire to

teach older children and to be able to teach more academic curriculum. I will be moving on from here. I'm sorry to have to leave, but I wish you all the best.

2012

During January of 2012, Maria experienced a serious fall that, looking back, may have had more serious physical consequences than we realized at the time. She was singing in the choir one Sunday at her church, and we found out later that she hadn't eaten breakfast that morning. As a result, during the third or fourth song, she fainted and fell face forward into the wooden floor. Everything stopped when it happened, and Barbara rushed to Maria's side. She was knocked out, but she recovered relatively soon, and since I was not there, Barbara and others moved Maria to the kitchen area and gave her some water and some nourishment. By the time the service ended, she appeared to be fully recovered, and she was not experiencing any of the symptoms of a concussion (headache, nausea, vomiting, or dizziness, among others).

Thus, on the surface, it seemed like a minor event, and maybe it was, but all these years later, I wonder if Maria experienced any long-term physical consequences as a result of that fall, consequences that could have negatively affected her health and well being down the road. I'll never know for sure, of course, but this is one of the many events in Maria's life that simply come to my mind periodically and leave me pondering them for the rest of the day.

  Since Maria no longer had a steady income from her day-care position and since no other teaching position appeared likely at that time, she began to look into a clerical position at a local hospital, a position that offered health care and retirement benefits. One of her two roommates worked in that hospital, and she told Maria about some of the openings there and encouraged Maria to apply. Almost four full years had passed since Maria's graduation from college, and I think she began to tire of struggling so much to find work and to pay her bills. She hadn't quite given up on her dream of working as a teacher, but she wasn't quite ready to take on more school debt for a master's degree, and she felt she needed a less stressful life and a chance to build up her savings account before she began taking graduate classes on a part-time basis. Thus, on May 21, she began working as an appointment secretary for an affiliated medical clinic near the hospital, a clinic that specialized in rheumatology and nutrition. There, she answered the phones, scheduled appointments, and assisted doctors, nurses, nutritionists, and diabetic educators.

  At first, I believe the job was a bit challenging for her because she sat at a desk and worked at a computer all day, quite a change from most of her previous job responsibilities. Once she settled into the position, though, she seemed more relaxed. The job was near where she lived, so she had a short commute; then, when the lease with her two friends expired, she and her hospital friend found another apartment even closer to the hospital. As a result of these changes in her work and living situation, Maria had more free time — and less financial stress — which allowed her to pursue other activities, and she continued to teach Sunday School classes at her church. Naturally, the Sunday School teaching filled her need for interactions with young people, and we all felt good about Maria's overall situation.

2013

About a year after securing her first job connected to the hospital, Maria applied for another job within the same hospital, a job that offered a bit more responsibility and a higher salary. Instead of merely scheduling appointments, she worked as a referral coordinator. The job's location was actually in the hospital, and she again had to answer the phone and schedule appointments, but she also had to make sure the patients completed their eligibility requirements, and she had to collaborate with other departments within the hospital to maintain consistent communication between those departments. This particular office also had more workers, young people like Maria, so I think she experienced even more camaraderie with them.

One new activity for Maria during this time was writing fiction. During her academic career, of course, she had written extensively on a variety of subjects, but most of those writings were essays or research papers or poems. Since she wasn't taking any classes at this point, she finally began to write a novel, the idea for which she had told me about previously. The novel was a family drama written for middle-school students, and the major event in the story would be the family's cross-country trip to visit the Grand Canyon. Though Maria never showed me her actual text, I did find the first 15 pages or so in a file on her computer after she passed. Her writing was pretty good, and I would have liked to have seen more of it, but the one part that totally surprised me was the dedication she had written up front:

> I'm honored to say that this is my first published book. My dad has encouraged me to write since I was a very young girl. As a young girl, I always admired my dad's loyalty, unconditional love, and his commitment to work, family, and others. His love of literature and writing was also passed down to me. This book is dedicated to my dad who inspired me to write. Thanks Dad! :) I love you.

Wow! What more can I say?

2014

2014 was a hard year for all of us. Barbara was struggling physically and had to be hospitalized for ten days early in the year, and the doctors determined that she had Hodgkin's lymphoma. As a result, she had to undergo months of chemotherapy treatments, and she lost all of her hair. In addition, she later went through both radiation and stem-cell replacement therapy. As you can imagine, Maria, Katrina, and I tried to be there for Barbara as much as we could, but Maria seemed especially worried, and the situation may have challenged her faith a bit. We found out later that Maria confided to Barbara's sister, Linda, that "It just isn't fair. Moms are supposed to take care of their children, not the other way around." Naturally, during that time, we all spent as much time with Barbara as we could, and we prayed constantly for her complete recovery. Fortunately, God answered those prayers, and Barbara is still cancer free to this day.

At the same time, my dad was in the midst of a medical struggle of his own. Previously, he had been diagnosed with pancreatic cancer. A widower in his late eighties, he decided he didn't want to go through any complicated treatments, and his next couple years were uneventful. His final year, 2014, though, was a struggle as he became extremely weak and slept often, so my four sisters and I took turns staying with him at his home during that time. That meant I spent at least one night per week with him and left Barbara home alone on her own. That wasn't ideal, of course, but Barbara understood, and she sometimes accompanied me when I went to stay with Dad.

Finally, in mid-June, Barbara and the girls and I, along with about a dozen other family members, were with Dad when he passed in his own bed. On that final night, he was unable to speak to us, he had a faraway look in his eyes, and he seemed to be reaching out to someone who we believe was welcoming him into heaven. Little did we know at that time that within a year and a half, we would experience a similar situation with our precious Maria.

In addition to those emotional family experiences, Maria was still lamenting some personal relationships that didn't work out. During Maria's time at college and the years afterwards, she interacted with many different young men on campus and in our local community when she returned home. Normally, she met her male friends through classes, through work, and through church activities such as Bible studies or entertaining field trips. Once again, I know she was seriously interested in one or two young men, and a few of her male friends expressed an interest in her, but only two of those relationships could be considered dating relationships. In both cases, Barbara and I met these young men and entertained them in our home with Maria, and, in fact, we met the parents of one of the young men. However, both relationships ended after a relatively short time. Thus, Maria was not in a serious relationship with anyone when she first began suffering from what she thought were severe migraine headaches.

2015

As I mentioned elsewhere, Maria left behind numerous examples of her writing: journals, essays, stories, and poems. The following is a poem entitled "I'll Always Remember," a poem she wrote when she was still in high school. The second-to-last stanza offers a challenge to the reader, one that is easy to write as a young person but difficult to live up to at any age but especially when one's plans and dreams have not yet been fulfilled. As you read through some of the comments following the poem, I think you'll see that Maria, despite her struggles and disappointments, still did her best to live up to her own expectations.

I'll Always Remember…

When I die
 and my funeral is nigh,
I want to be remembered
As the one who said "Hi" to everyone, and
Was always kind, friendly, and caring.

Days pass by; good and bad,
Good-hair days and bad,
Days when I feel ugly
And days when I feel like hot stuff,
but
no day passes where there isn't the opportunity
To show my love to someone else.

When you're remembered,
Will you be known as lazy
Or as the one who couldn't be stopped
No matter what?

Did every tough time bring you down?

Take the challenge and
Show kindness each and every day.

You are not defined by clothes
Or hairstyles, but, instead,
By your daily actions.

Maria's final full year on this earth was spent working at her full-time job at the hospital, and from what I can tell, she worked really well in that position and was appreciated by her peers. In fact, after she passed and I was going through all of her papers, I found two notes that came from her co-workers, notes that I assume were initiated by her supervisor to allow everyone to explain the positive traits that they appreciated about one another.

One short, specific note mentioned that Maria was "always positive and cheerful when most needed." The other note was a collection of ten attributes, and each one was written in a different handwriting with different ink, leading me to believe that everyone in the department contributed to these sheets of positive attributes for one another. Maria's list included the following words or phrases: "positive, hard worker, excellent phone skills, nice, helpful, very thoughtful and kind, sweet, caring, very cool, and friendly."

While doing her best in her full-time position as a referral coordinator, Maria was also preparing for her eventual departure from that job, so she would be better qualified to finally obtain a full-time teaching position. In one of her journals, in fact, she lamented her office job because although she had some financial security, she really wanted to be a full-time teacher: "I used to teach children to share, to write, and do arithmetic. Now, I answer phones and sit at a computer five days a week." As a result, she spent the spring of 2015 applying to graduate schools and completing all the necessary requirements such as securing letters of recommendation and writing her philosophy of education among others. In one of her application documents, I found the following sentences that give a small glimpse into the way Maria viewed her responsibilities as a teacher.

"I will simply treat every student with love and respect. No one student will be viewed as better. I will show love and respect to all students who enter my classroom, and I will expect the same from them. I will value all students by finding their strengths and praising them for these strengths regularly."

Consequently, by mid summer, Maria had been accepted into a graduate program at a nearby university, and she signed up to take two courses. She was so excited. She couldn't wait to get started. Five months later, after Maria passed away, one of her graduate classmates wrote about those first few days in the program:

> I met Maria at orientation; we sat at the same table with others. We spent a piece of the day together, went to the bookstore together, and sat by the fountain for an hour just talking

about how much she wanted to be a teacher. She had been out of the teaching world for a little bit, working in a hospital, but I could easily see how excited she was to get back into education. I could just see that passion. We talked about church and her involvement with Sunday School. She was just so kind. Later in the semester, if I'd had a bad day, even though we didn't really know each other that well, she was supportive and would give me the space I needed, and she was there to listen. Maria was a truly kind soul.

Then, the semester itself proved to be a real challenge for Maria. I don't think she realized initially how time-consuming the two graduate classes — and all the readings and the homework — would be on top of her full-time job. In addition, she had a new laptop that she was using to write all of her school papers, and for some reason, the word-processing program wasn't working properly. Still, she persevered.

Naturally, because of her busy schedule, Barbara and Katrina and I didn't see her as often, but I usually saw her for just a few minutes each Monday, late in the afternoon.

Coincidentally, I was teaching a writing course for employees at the hospital where Maria worked, and my class began at 5:00 p.m., just a bit later than when Maria finished her normal workday before heading out to her own class. Thus, I would typically arrive a bit early and sit in a small café near where her department was located. She would see me on her way out the door, and we would share a few moments of conversation together before we each ran off to our classes. Looking back, those moments were so brief, but I like to think that we encouraged one another to not get too caught up in the busyness of life and, instead, to stop and enjoy our precious moments with loved ones, or as Maria said in her poem, "to show kindness each and every day."

Our Sweet Maria — Her Final 30 Days

Christmas Eve
Thursday, December 24

On Christmas Eve, we planned to go to the service at our church. Maria had come from the house she shared with friends to our home, and she was going to stay overnight and spend Christmas morning with us as we normally did, opening presents and later spending the day with Barbara's entire family. Our niece Laura and her husband, Rob, had volunteered to host the gathering at their new home.

Maria, however, was not feeling well. On the previous Saturday, the 19th, she was supposed to attend a play with a friend, but she didn't feel up to it, so she stayed at her place. She was suffering from what she described as a "terrible migraine headache," a first for her. At times, too, she had experienced nausea and vomiting. Since Maria had often experienced back pain (perhaps as a result of a fainting spell and subsequent fall years earlier), I think she felt the headache was purely a physical consequence of the back pain, and that some physical therapy might correct the problem. Since she had also just completed her first six credits in a master's-degree program in addition to working full-time, I think we all believed that the stress of her work and her education may have contributed to her problem as well.

Her pain became so bad that she visited her primary doctor and her chiropractor on the following

Monday, her 30th birthday — December 21st. The chiropractor worked on her back and neck a bit, and her primary doctor gave her an injection to ease the pain. Those treatments seemed to help her in the short term, but soon, she was suffering again.

On Tuesday the 22nd and Wednesday the 23rd, she called in sick for work, and when the pain seemed to get even worse, we took her to a nearby urgent-care facility on Wednesday evening. After Maria explained everything to the doctor on duty, he ordered a CT scan, the medical people performed "intravenous therapy," and he also gave her an IV and some medication, to take at home. The CT scan didn't show anything, so the doctor agreed with Maria's diagnosis that she had a serious migraine, and he seemed confident that the medications would help her. Thus, we brought Maria to our home confident and optimistic that Maria's headache would gradually go away.

Even though Maria was still in pain the next day, she was determined to attend the Christmas Eve services that night, so we went to church, and we sat in the last row of chairs just in case we needed to bring her home early. And somehow, Maria made it through the service.

I sat on one side of her, and the two of us remained seated for most of the service, even during the congregational singing when everyone else stood. Maria rested her head on my shoulder for much of the service, and she fidgeted and fussed from time to time as she tried to find the most comfortable position.

Though I cannot speak for Maria, I like to think that she was comforted by the familiarity of the service and the place and the annual church rituals. We always sing lots of traditional Christmas carols, we have special Christmas songs performed by our own worship team, we have a Christmas message from our pastor, and at the end, we always turn down all the lights, so that the sanctuary is completely dark except for one solitary candle on the altar representing the symbolic light of Jesus Christ and His birth in the stable.

From that single candle, our pastor lights a smaller candle which he holds, and, then, he uses it to light two more small candles, one held by an usher on one side of the church and another held by a second usher on the other side. These ushers then carry their candles to the people standing at the end of each row, and these people pass the flame to those next to them. And while the church is gradually being filled by the light of Christ, we are all singing "Silent Night."

When our girls were little, this candle ritual was their favorite part of the Christmas Eve service, and we had to watch closely to make sure that they didn't burn themselves with the flame or get hot wax on their skin as they lit their candles and passed the light on to others.

On this particular night, poor Maria was feeling too weak to hold a candle, but she appeared to be watching everything, and again I like to think that she was recalling the Christmases of her youth and enjoying that experience again.

After the singing ended and the pastor gave the final benediction, most people began to socialize a bit before filing out of the church. While Maria remained seated, I stood and greeted some friends, knowing that we would leave soon as a family. As Maria was waiting, though, a man she did not know approached her and began speaking to her. We discovered later that he was the husband of a girl older than Maria who had also grown up in our church. This girl's new family lived in Virginia and had returned to visit her parents and their extended family for Christmas, and they had been sitting in a row of extra chairs against the back wall of the sanctuary, separated from us by only about six feet of space where people filed in from the center row to the side rows.

When this man approached Maria, he spoke to her for just a minute or so and gave her a small gift. Maria was so touched by that act of kindness and compassion that she later posted this message on Facebook:

> Random acts of kindness are a blessing. Normally, I love to bless others, but last night, someone blessed me with a random act of kindness. For the past week, I've been suffering from an intense migraine. Although I didn't feel well, I wanted to attend our Christmas Eve service at church with my family. I was experiencing a lot of pain, and it showed all across my face. I sat during the service and enjoyed listening to each song and verse shared throughout the service. It was a blessing to be there and prayed for by friends despite my intense pain. Thank you, everyone. At the end of the service, a man came up to me and said, 'I don't know you, but I could tell you were having a hard night and wanted to give you this. I'm a cop, and I give these to people I interact with during my work.' It was an engraved, silver coin bigger than a quarter with a Crown on one side

and a cross with a Bible verse from Psalm 46:10 on the other: 'Be still and know that I am God.' Thank you for blessing me. It truly put a smile on my face. Merry Christmas, Everyone!

Usually, when we leave the church after our Christmas Eve service, we don't go directly home. Instead, our tradition is to drive not on the main highway but on the secondary roads and through neighborhoods, so we can observe and admire all the Christmas lights and decorations that businesses and families put up to brighten the dark December nights.

We usually drive past one business in particular because it offers a gigantic display of lights spread over its property: Santa and his elves, the reindeer and Santa's sled filled with gifts, a big Christmas tree, a manger scene with Joseph, Mary, and the baby Jesus plus lots of miscellaneous decorations that go on and off, so it appears as if children and animals are actually moving about on a playground. Each year, the display is a little bigger and better, and even though our girls were 30 and 27 at that point, we always enjoyed this wonderful spectacle.

After we viewed that display, we would typically drive through a collection of neighborhoods to see other displays of lights on houses and in front yards. The lawn displays range from snowmen and reindeer to mangers and the "Grinch Who Stole Christmas." Naturally, too, many homes have lighted icicles hanging from the roofs with lots of additional lights on all the trees and bushes in the yards.

One of our favorite displays, though, is the simple collection of small luminary candles in white paper bags held down by sand. These luminaries usually line driveways or stretch from one house to the next. Certain neighborhoods appear to have almost total participation, and driving through these streets is a magical experience, one we enjoy year after year.

On this particular Christmas Eve, however, we decided to go straight home from church because Maria still felt so bad; we told ourselves that we could go on another night. Yes, the luminaries would be gone, but most of the other lights and decorations would be on display at least until New Year's Day.

Christmas Day
Friday, December 25

Though Maria and Katrina both had their own places, they spent Christmas Eve at our house and slept over. On Christmas morning, we usually all sleep late, and no one opens any presents until everyone is awake and downstairs. Even when the girls were little, they didn't get up early. Usually, Barbara was the first one awake, anxiously waiting for the rest of us. This day was no different.

When we finally gathered together in the living room near the tree, Maria seemed to be in about the same condition as the night before. Despite the medications, her headache persisted. She sat on the love seat near the window, and we brought her presents to her, mostly clothes as I recall.

Then, after we ate breakfast and began to get ready for the day ahead, Maria decided that she wasn't feeling strong enough to go out, so she would stay home by herself.

"I'll stay with you, Sweetheart," I volunteered immediately. "I don't like Barbara's family anyway," I joked.

"No, it's okay, Dad," she responded. "I'll be okay, and if I'm not, I'll call you."

Since the gathering was only 10-15 minutes from our house, I consented, but I added, "You better call me if you need me."

"I will, Dad. Don't worry."

Another Christmas tradition in our family is taking a picture of the girls — both separately and together — next to the Christmas tree. I began this tradition after Maria was born on December 21, 1985. On Christmas Day of that year, I settled our precious, little angel in our portable baby carrier and set the carrier under the Christmas tree in our first apartment and took her picture.

Only four days old, Maria was wearing a red, hooded outfit, and all we could see of her was her face and a little bit of her brown hair. She appeared to be looking off to the side, at her mother perhaps, with a puzzled and inquisitive expression on her face as if to say, "Where am I, and what is going on here?"

Since that first Christmas with Maria, I have always said that she is the best Christmas present I ever received, and every year since Maria's birth, I have continued with the Christmas photos. I usually take the pictures just before we leave the house to attend a family gathering, or, on the days when we hosted, just before anyone was scheduled to arrive. The girls were always dressed up for the special day, and in some of the annual photos, they are wearing one of their presents or holding a special gift they received that day. Again, however, because Maria wasn't feeling well and wasn't planning on leaving the house, I didn't take any pictures that morning. Just as I assumed we'd have another chance to view Christmas lights in the neighborhoods, I also assumed I'd have another chance to take pictures of the girls near the tree a day or two later. Needless to say, I never had the chance to take any 2015 pictures. That Christmas morning was the last morning Maria ever spent in our home. We brought her to the hospital later that day, and she never came home again.

Around 2:00 p.m., Barbara, Katrina, and I left to attend the family gathering. By then, Maria had bathed and eaten, but she still felt weak, so we left her sitting on the couch in the living room with the television remote and her telephone and an admonition to "Please call us if you need anything, anything at all."
She was trying to be strong, of course, because that's what Maria always did, and she didn't want any of us to miss the party, so she again assured us that she'd be okay and that she would, indeed, call if she needed anything.
So we drove to the party with two cars just in case and spent the next three hours visiting with Barbara's parents, her three siblings and their spouses, and with most of her siblings' children as well, a total of about 20 people.
"Where's Maria?" Everyone asked, of course.

"She's not feeling well," I responded. "She's never had a migraine before, but she's had one now for over four days, and it won't go away." Then, I explained about the doctor visits and the medications, and everyone commiserated and shared their own headache stories or the headache sagas of someone they knew. And of course, when we don't have a headache ourselves, we forget how annoying and painful it can be, especially if it has dragged on for a while.

By 5:00 p.m., we had polished off a round of drinks and hors d'oeuvres, and we had also finished dinner and were looking forward to dessert when Maria called me on my cell phone.

"Hi, Sweetie. What's up? Are you okay?"

"Yes, but would you come home and be with me. I just need some company."

"Of course, Angel. I'll leave right now. Do you want Mom and Katrina too?"

"No. They can stay."

"Alright, Baby. I'm leaving now."

As I began saying a quick good-bye to everyone, our hostess, Maria's cousin Laura and her mother put together a plate of food and dessert for me to take to Maria. Everyone expressed their concern for Maria, and within ten minutes, I was on my way home. I wasn't overly nervous or concerned because Maria had sounded okay on the phone. I assumed the two of us would chat for a while and maybe watch some television together before Barbara and Katrina returned later. When I got home, though, Maria was not doing as well as she had professed earlier on the phone.

"My head still hurts," she admitted quickly, "and now my neck hurts too. Would you massage my temples and my neck?"

"Of course, Angel. Of course."

Though Maria had never experienced headache pain this intense and for such a long time before, she had always struggled with chronic pain in her back, so I often gave her massages. On this day, as she lay on her back on the couch, I placed my two middle fingers on her temples and gently made small circles to try and ease her suffering. After a while, she turned over onto her stomach and asked me to apply finger pressure to her neck, at about ear level, and gently push downward. I spent about 10-15 minutes between the two activities, and she seemed to relax a bit before she asked me to stop. Then, she turned over again to face me and sit up.

"Dad," she said, as if she wanted to say more, but before she continued, she seemed about to fall off the couch. I caught her and asked, "Maria, are you okay?"

She had a faraway look in her eyes, and I knew something was wrong.

As I held her, I quickly called Katrina, who is a physician assistant, for guidance. Maria did not pass out, but she was a bit wobbly, and she finally said,

"Dad, I can't see very well."

"Call an ambulance," Katrina said immediately when I explained Maria's loss of vision. "We'll be right there."

I nervously called 911 and explained what was going on and prepared to accompany Maria to the hospital. Despite her condition, she was more calm than I was. She specifically asked for certain shoes and a particular jacket. I think knowing that she was going to get help may have relieved some of the pain and stress she was experiencing.

The ambulance arrived, and two young men quickly evaluated Maria and prepared her for transport. Just as they placed her on the stretcher and headed for the door, Barbara and Katrina arrived and reassured her as well as they could.

"You're going to be okay, Maria," Katrina said.

"We'll be right behind you," Barbara added.

The men in the ambulance were wonderful. I had hoped to sit in the back with Maria, but the driver said that was against regulations; he quickly added, however, that I would be able to see Maria and talk to her from the passenger seat up front, and sure enough, an opening there allowed me to peek into the rear of the ambulance to see and hear what was going on, and I was able to listen to her attendant and also talk to her as the driver transported us to the hospital.

Quite honestly, though, I didn't have to say much because the young man in the back was so kind to her and kept her fully engaged in conversation, which I'm sure also took her mind off her pain. He asked her questions about what she was feeling and about what had been happening to her during the previous week. Then, he also asked her about where she worked and where she had gone to school. Maria wasn't quite as animated as she was normally when she met someone for the first time. Still, she sounded good, and I felt optimistic, despite my concern over what had just happened, that we would get Maria all the help she needed and quickly bring her home.

After all, I had recently endured a similar ambulance ride just two weeks earlier. I was helping a student in The Writing Center at our community college when I felt my heartbeat begin to race. Part of me wanted to ignore it and hope it would go away, but another part of me worried that I was having a heart attack. Since I wasn't having any chest pain, I walked to the nearby health center, and the nurse there checked my pulse and called an ambulance immediately. Fortunately, within minutes, my racing heartbeat returned to normal; unfortunately, the nurse and the ambulance staff agreed that they wanted me to be checked out thoroughly, so they brought me to the emergency room, and the doctor there suggested I stay overnight for observation. In fact, Maria and Katrina both gave up their planned Friday-night activities to sit with Barbara and me in the hospital. That night, I slept comfortably, my heartbeat never accelerated again, and by noon the next day, they released me. Based on what I had told them, the doctors theorized that I may have experienced end-of-semester stress, and my heart simply reacted in an unusual way that had passed quickly.

Thus, as the ambulance carrying Maria approached the same hospital where I had been examined and cared for, I felt confident that the staff there would provide Maria with similar care, even if her situation were a bit more complicated. This was also the same hospital where Maria worked. The doctor in the emergency room would evaluate her, and they might keep her overnight, but I knew they would figure out what was wrong with Maria and send her home with a treatment plan as well.

As I mentioned previously, my assumptions were so wrong. Maria would spend the next 26 days in that hospital before being transferred to the Hospice wing of another hospital where she spent the final four days of her life. I survived my minor health scare, but poor Maria would not survive what she thought was a migraine headache.

Christmas Night
Friday, December 25

We arrived in the emergency room sometime between 6:00 and 6:30. During her time there, Maria experienced some of the same procedures I went through just two weeks earlier. They examined her and hooked her up to a heart monitor to track her heartbeat, and it was a bit slow. They also asked her lots of questions about what she had experienced prior to coming into the hospital. Naturally, too, Maria described the pain in her head and neck as "throbbing" and "severe," a seven out of ten. She said she had back pain also. In addition to the head, neck, and back pain, Maria felt nauseous, lightheaded, and experienced some vomiting.

Regarding her vision, she actually lost the vision in her right eye for about three minutes at a time, and it happened three or four times. Maria remained in the ER for two hours or so as various medical people examined her before they transferred her to the neurology wing on the fifth floor by about 8:00 to

8:30, and there, with some medication, she began to settle in for the night.

The fact that they wanted Maria to stay overnight did not bother me at all. In fact, I was comforted and relieved. For just as they had me stay overnight after my racing-heartbeat episode, they were advising Maria to do the same. Thus, I expected them to run some tests on her, figure out what was wrong, and send her home with either medications that would relieve her pain or with a specific diagnosis of the problem and a treatment plan. At that time, too, I think I realized that Maria might need more than one night or two. After all, her problem, whatever it was, had already been present for a week, and the medical staff might need more time with her, especially with her intermittent loss of vision in one eye.

I was also comforted by the medical people we met that evening. The main nurse responsible for that neurology room seemed friendly, attentive, and professional. She assured us that Maria would be in good hands, and we did not need to stay overnight in the hospital with Maria. We could go home and get a good night's rest. So that's exactly what we did. We stayed until about 10:00, and once we felt that Maria was somewhat comfortable, we went home: Barbara and I to our place and Katrina to her apartment. We all promised that we would return early the next morning.

Saturday, December 26

On Saturday the 26th, Barbara and Katrina returned to the hospital early that morning around 8:00, but I did not. Instead, I spent most of the day with my nephew David because he had agreed earlier that week to help me move some of Maria's stuff from the house that she was sharing with friends to an apartment that she was going to share with Katrina in another city. Maria's plan was to have her stuff moved by January 1st, and since David owned a pickup truck, he and I filled his truck and my SUV with her boxes of books and clothes and other assorted possessions and made one trip to the new apartment. We planned another trip for her furniture prior to the end of December.

As I recall, that first hospital room was situated on the left end of the hall on the neurology wing and had two beds, one of which was unoccupied, so that's where I went during that late afternoon. The girls filled me in on what had occurred that day, and I updated them on the work David and I had done.

For Maria, numerous doctors had examined her physically with various tests. An ophthalmology specialist also came in to check her vision. In addition, they scheduled her for a lumbar puncture to relieve some excess fluid from her spine and reduce the pain in her back. At one point, Maria's headache seemed to have disappeared, but it later returned with some dizziness. The doctors also recommended a psychiatric consult to make sure Maria wasn't just imagining the pain and another ophthalmology consult due to the loss of vision in her right eye. After an hour or so, I visited the cafeteria downstairs for some nourishment, and when I returned, probably 30 to 40 minutes later, Maria was no longer in that first room.

Unfortunately, about 20 minutes before I returned, Maria experienced a seizure in that room, a code blue, and she was immediately moved to another room on that same wing where they could treat her for that emergency and monitor her condition more closely.

When the seizure occurred, Barbara was in the room with her sister, Linda, and Katrina, and when Maria began convulsing in her bed, they called for help immediately. According to Barbara, the convulsions continued for about four minutes while the medical staff worked on Maria. Barbara said the seizure was so difficult to witness that she had to look out the window instead. Once the code-blue team of about eight professionals finally stabilized Maria, they decided to move her.

The second room was much bigger than the first and included about eight beds with lots of additional equipment around each bed, so the medical staff stationed in that large room could more easily monitor all of her vital functions. We had to wait outside while they connected all the equipment, and though we asked what caused the seizure, they were unable to tell us anything at that point. Fortunately, Maria's condition had stabilized by later that night, and, again, they encouraged us to go home and get some rest because Maria would be fine, especially with all the added equipment and additional medical personnel to check on her.

Sunday, December 27

Normally, we would go to church on Sunday morning, but, naturally, we went to see Maria instead. Apparently, she slept well with no problems and with no indications that she had such a difficult day on Saturday. Thank God.

On this day, they performed a third test of her heartbeat, and the results were similar to those from previous days: her heartbeat was still a bit slow, but, otherwise, everything was normal.

They performed a lumbar puncture to remove some excess fluid from her spinal cord, and when they tested that fluid, the results showed some inflammation. After that procedure, Maria indicated that her back felt less painful as a result, but the doctors still had not figured out what exactly was wrong and what was also causing her headache and her neck pain.

Perhaps because it was a Sunday on Christmas weekend, the whole floor seemed a bit quieter than the previous two days. By then, I was hopeful, and praying, that on Monday, Maria would see a medical person who had a bit more insight into what was going on with her.

Also that afternoon, a hospital chaplain visited because Maria had experienced that code-blue seizure a day earlier. The chaplain spoke to us and to Maria for a while. He also offered to pray and said he would be available for assistance as needed. Since we didn't know this gentleman at all and since we couldn't get a good feel for his religious beliefs, we were polite and respectful, but we didn't really open up to him as we might have if he had come from our church or the church that Maria attended.

Monday, December 28

As I hoped, various medical professionals visited Maria on this day and examined her. Unfortunately, we still didn't know anything for sure about the major problem. With each test the doctors performed on Maria, they suspected a certain cause or a possible problem. For instance, they mentioned the possibility of multiple sclerosis because of the inflammation of her optic nerve. Yet the results up to that point had not indicated any particular reason for Maria's problems. Yes, the diagnostic process was frustrating.

Despite her discomfort and during all of the tests, Maria appeared to be holding up pretty well. She didn't show her frustration, and she was friendly and polite and appreciative to everyone. Typical Maria.

For those of us sitting with her, we tried to take her mind off the situation by reading to her, listening to music, and simply talking to her about more pleasant subjects: her friends, her graduate courses, her church, anything to distract her. In fact, one of the highlights of each day occurred when the nurse dropped off a menu, and Maria was allowed to choose what she wanted for her next meal. Quite honestly, she wasn't even eating that much because, under the circumstances, she didn't have much of an appetite, but she still seemed to enjoy the choosing conversation, and on one occasion, she saw something that she thought I might enjoy, and she asked, "Should I order that for you, Dad?" What a sweetheart.

In the meantime, I felt somewhat guilty because I had my own stupid and selfish thoughts. At times on Sunday, for instance, I was honestly thinking more about the New York Jets than I was my own precious daughter. They were playing the hated New England Patriots, and, believe it or not, the Jets still had a chance to make the playoffs, something they hadn't done for a long time.

Maria knew I'm a big Jets fan, and, in fact, all four of us went down to The Meadowlands three years earlier to see them play; they lost that day, naturally. So when Maria realized on the 27th that it was Sunday afternoon, she asked me if the Jets were playing, and when she found out they were, she told me to go ahead and put the television on, so we could watch. She was in and out, of course, and not really paying attention, but I think she liked the familiarity of watching the game together, and she was happy for me when the Jets won, a bright moment on an otherwise dreary day in the hospital. (No surprise; the Jets lost the following week and did not make the playoffs.)

Tuesday, December 29

This was another day of tests for Maria. She endured multiple CT scans of the abdomen and pelvis and also of the head and neck. The doctors were concerned about sarcoidosis (enlargement of lymph nodes) versus lymphoma (cancer of the lymph nodes). Fortunately, the CT scans did not uncover any major problems.

In addition, Maria endured inpatient visits from three different doctors: one from neurology, one from cardiology, and one from oncology. The oncology doctor mentioned that Maria had "facial paralysis" on both sides, though, quite honestly, I had not noticed. Looking back, I wonder if I failed to notice because I was too close to Maria in the hospital, spending almost every waking hour of every day with her. Her health was apparently deteriorating right in front of me, but my optimistic nature failed to see it. Finally, the medical people also performed two more ECGs; the first ECG indicated a "slow heartbeat," and the second indicated an "irregular heart rhythm"; neither one merited any additional attention from the doctors.

Later on this day, they moved Maria to another section of this big room, from a bed in the middle of the large room with eight beds to a much smaller room with only one bed, a room that was a bit more isolated and quieter. I think they did this because Maria had stabilized quite a bit. That, at least, was a positive sign, and as Maria's family members, we were relieved to have much more privacy with her.

Wednesday, December 30

We were gradually falling into a discouraging routine at this point. Every day, Barbara and I drove from our home to arrive at the hospital at about 8:00 when Maria had her breakfast. Katrina couldn't visit every day because she was working most days as a physician assistant at the other major hospital nearby. Fortunately, Barbara and I were free because my school had been on semester break since the three days before Christmas, and Barbara had her own coaching business, and she typically didn't see many clients during the holidays. Unfortunately, all of us felt like we were treading water with no idea if we were floating into deeper waters or moving toward the safety of shore.

On this day, for example, the regular doctors came in and examined Maria with their normal tests. They looked into her eyes, her ears, and her mouth, and, apparently, everything looked okay. They prodded and poked her body a bit to see how she reacted. Then, they held her hands and asked her to push and pull, and they did something similar with her feet to test her strength and her resistance. Naturally, too, they checked her charts, her pulse, and her blood pressure, and they asked the same questions every day: "Did you sleep okay? How do you feel? Where's the pain? On a scale of 1 to 10, what is it?" (Usually, it was between 5 and 7.) And on and on and on.

Poor Maria was a real trooper, and she politely answered their questions and endured their examinations, but when she asked, "What's wrong?" they didn't have a satisfying answer. They typically had a theory or a suspicion, so they would tell her that they were going to test for that idea, but that just meant more waiting. And this particular day was definitely a waiting day.

The only real change involved the doctors. One neurology doctor, who knew Katrina well and had been seeing Maria since she arrived, notified us that this day was his last day because he and his family were moving to Florida for a new position. That was a real disappointment for us because even though he hadn't yet come up with a diagnosis for Maria, he was always especially kind and helpful and had gone out of his way to make sure Maria had whatever she needed to be as comfortable as possible despite her difficult situation. In fact, one day, when Maria needed a particular procedure and the assigned person wasn't performing that task in a timely manner, this doctor just jumped in and did it himself. Thus, though we wished him well in his new endeavor, we knew we would definitely miss him.

The other small change occurred when Barbara's oncology doctor came in to check on Maria. As I mentioned previously, in 2014, Barbara endured a long battle with cancer, Hodgkin's lymphoma. As a result, she, too, was in the hospital for over a week as the doctors analyzed her situation, and once they figured it out, Barbara successfully went through months of chemotherapy treatments, and she lost all of her hair. In addition, she later went through both radiation and stem-cell replacement therapy. This particular doctor was with Barbara through most of her sessions, so we knew her well and felt comfortable with her. Consequently, despite our frustration of not having a diagnosis, this doctor's arrival reminded us that just as Barbara survived her medical struggle,

Maria, too, would fight — and survive — through her battle, whatever it was.

New Year's Eve
Thursday, December 31

New Year's Eve has always been a special day in our family. In fact, I would say that our family of four began on New Year's Eve as 1983 turned into 1984. Barbara and I had been dating for only about half a year at that time, but I knew by then that I wanted to marry her. Thus, as 1984 approached, I brought Barbara to a house party with the plan of proposing to her right after midnight, so we could officially start the New Year together. I didn't propose to her in front of everyone, though. Instead, we exited the party shortly after exchanging a New Year's kiss, and I proposed to her back at her apartment. Obviously, she said, "Yes," and we have bored the girls with that romantic tale every year on New Year's Eve since then.

In subsequent years, we always stayed at home as a family and watched a movie and ate junk food. Though Barbara and Maria would often fall asleep after the movie, Katrina and I would usually stay up and watch the festivities from New York City as the Times Square Ball dropped at midnight. As 2015 began to fade into 2016, we knew we wouldn't watch a movie or stay up till midnight. This last day of 2015 was much like the day before.

A few doctors visited to check on Maria, but the whole floor seemed quiet, as if everyone were moving in slow motion, much like the caricature of the crotchety old man who represented the previous year who was about to give way to the child who represented the upcoming year.

Katrina came by after work, as she did on most days, and she mentioned that some of her co-workers were going out later to celebrate the arrival of 2016. Barbara and I could tell that she was torn between staying with Maria and going out, so we encouraged her to do a little bit of both. Maria, too, told her basically the same thing. The previous week had been hard on all of us, but especially on Katrina because she was taking care of others all day, every day, and, then, trying to do what she could for her sister in the evenings. Though Barbara, Maria, and I knew we wouldn't actually be going out, I think we all felt as if we might experience the night vicariously through Katrina. Thus, she stayed with Maria until about 8:30 or 9:00 and, then, left to be with her friends. Barbara and I stayed for an hour afterwards before we kissed Maria good-night and headed home. All three of us were in bed and sleeping as the rest of the world ushered in the new year.

Friday, January 1

The New Year — 2016 — arrived, but Maria was still in the hospital, still with no diagnosis.

Her vital signs on this day were stable, but the doctors still could not figure out what was causing all of Maria's pain. One of the doctors explained that it might possibly be caused by inflammation of the nerves in her brain which could also affect the nerves in her face and eyes. In addition, she was still having trouble seeing out of her right eye. That same doctor also explained that in addition to the inflammation of the nerves in her brain, an infection in her brain could be a possibility.

He also believed Maria's problems could have been neurological, according to her symptoms, but other possibilities existed as well, such as lymphoma, meningitis, lyme disease, tuberculosis, and sarcoidosis. The results of an MRI appeared normal.

The doctor performed another lumbar puncture to relieve some of the pressure from the excess fluid on her brain and spine, fluid which they theorized could be causing the pain. After that test, however, Maria noticed a new pain at the back of her head. The doctor said this could have been a consequence of the lumbar puncture. He suggested that Maria lie down flat in bed to reduce the pain, and he claimed her body would self correct by producing more fluid to replace what was drained away. As a consequence of the lumbar puncture, Maria's fluid level was low, and the doctors predicted that the correction might take a couple days.

As Maria's dad, watching her day-in and day-out, I felt like this experience was a bit of a roller coaster. Every time they performed a test or procedure, my hopes soared, and I wanted to believe that they would discover the problem and offer a solution in the form of a treatment plan. Naturally, when the test results failed to produce any clear direction, my hopes returned to earth, shattered and broken. We had been in the hospital with Maria for a week, and we still didn't have a diagnosis. In fact, one doctor began to refer to her as a "diagnostic dilemma." Obviously, that statement was not very encouraging, and I began to seriously question my optimism.

As a result, I began to worry that Maria's problem might be much more serious than I imagined, and I began to worry that we could lose her. When these thoughts occurred, though, I tried to overcome them with prayer. "Please take care of her, Lord," I prayed. "She's your little girl. Please help her through this ordeal. Please relieve her pain. Please help the doctors, the nurses, and all those involved in her care to figure out what is going on, and please intervene, so that she can begin to recover."

And speaking of nurses, one of the male nurses reported to us when we arrived on this day that Maria had been choking on coffee earlier, and that she was having more and more trouble swallowing her food. Then, in our presence, he reminded Maria to eat slowly, to always sit up when drinking, and to make sure she was fully awake when she ate or drank.

As a result of Maria's struggle to swallow, everyone on the medical staff recommended that she choose food that didn't require a lot of chewing, food that would go down easily. So for lunch, Maria ordered ground beef, mashed potatoes, and mushed up broccoli, and she ate about half of it. She also drank more of a chocolate supplement with extra protein. After lunch, she fell asleep, around 2:10.

While Maria slept, one of the doctors suggested that perhaps a speech specialist be brought in the next day, not so much because Maria was having trouble speaking but, instead, to allow the specialist to put a stethoscope on Maria's throat to listen as she ate different types of food. Such a test might explain why swallowing had suddenly become so difficult for her. Part of me wanted to believe that such a test might help, but a bigger part of me was concerned that the swallowing problem, on top of her pain and her vision problems, might just be another negative indicator of Maria's overall situation, another descent on the roller coaster.

Saturday, January 2

As suggested previously, a speech specialist visited Maria. This female doctor listened to Maria's throat with a stethoscope as Maria ate all of the following: apple sauce, thick cranberry juice through a straw, water through a straw, and a small bite of a tuna-fish sandwich.

After the test, the doctor spoke to Maria for a bit and concluded that Maria was swallowing well, but when she ate foods that required a lot of chewing, that experience tired her out. Thus, like the others, this doctor recommended only food that was easy to chew and swallow. She also suggested that when Maria ate, she should start with the more difficult foods, so she definitely would get some nourishment in her. Then, if she tired while eating, she could switch to the softer foods and drinks. Finally, Maria also needed to avoid food such as crackers, salads, and cookies or any other food that would be too much of a chore for her to swallow or that might cause her to choke. Before the doctor left, she said that she would check on Maria again later in the week.

    Obviously, I am not a doctor, but I, too, had noticed that Maria's ability to chew and to swallow had deteriorated during the week that she had been in the hospital. As mentioned previously, during the first few days, as we helped Maria choose her meals for the next day, the selection of the food and the actual meal times were a welcome diversion for Maria from the boredom and monotony of sitting in a hospital bed all day. Those diversions also helped to distract Maria from the pain she was feeling in her head, neck, and lower back. As the days passed, however, the meal times became more of a chore because it took so long for her to chew and to swallow. Also, I have to admit, that as I watched Maria eat on her own or as I helped to feed her, I began to worry that she was going to choke on something. I probably shouldn't have worried too much about that because, after all, we were surrounded by professionals who could help her quickly and efficiently. Still, I worried.

    Another doctor, a neurosurgeon this time, visited Maria later, and he physically examined Maria while Katrina was present. He noticed that Maria had some swollen lymph nodes on her neck and arm pits that could indicate an infection. Then, he mentioned the possible use of steroids to decrease the swelling, but he explained that steroids for Maria would probably not be a good idea because the steroids might make it more difficult to determine the major cause of Maria's problems. He also seemed to indicate that cancer was a possibility, so they would test for it.

As I mentioned earlier, the word "cancer" did not frighten me. In fact, I felt somewhat comforted by the word — if comfort is, indeed, possible in Maria's situation — because a diagnosis could lead to a plan of treatment. By contrast, the uncertainty sounded more ominous and more troublesome. I also felt that Maria's cancer situation might have been better than Barbara's situation. After all, Maria was much younger than Barbara, Barbara seemed to have been in a more delicate situation before they discovered her Hodgkin's lymphoma and began to treat it, and the whole cancer situation was new to us when it hit Barbara. Now that we had all been through it with her, I think we all — immediate and extended family and friends — felt confident that the medical professionals would discover what was wrong with Maria and figure out a way to fix it. Maria would be okay. We just needed some time.

Sunday, January 3

Today was another really quiet day with the normal doctor visits and no real progress or new information. I felt like we were all just waiting on test results, but honestly I had lost track of the tests and what their results might indicate. I was definitely out of my element.

As one of three family members accompanying Maria through this ordeal, I felt the least qualified to be of assistance. Her sister, Katrina, is a physician assistant, so she knew and understood pretty much everything that was going on when the doctors checked Maria and performed various tests and procedures. In fact, Barbara and I relied heavily on Katrina to explain most of the complicated medical information to us.

Barbara doesn't have the medical knowledge that Katrina has, but Barbara is a phenomenal communicator who is comfortable talking to everyone and asking lots of questions. As a result, she was a great advocate for Maria, and she made sure that Maria had everything she needed, and she also made sure that we understood everything that was going on.

So what was my role in Maria's care? I tried to absorb the medical information when Katrina was not present, and I tried to advocate for Maria when Barbara was away from Maria's hospital room. Mostly, though, I tried to comfort Maria by reading to her, by singing to her, or by finding music for her to listen to on her phone or on her computer. During her hospital stay, up to this point, she had watched very little television. She would much rather talk to us or listen to music or be read to since she didn't have the strength to read by herself.

As much as I could, I tried to help Maria feel comfortable or, at the least, somewhat distracted from her pain. That meant I adjusted her pillows, or I hit the button on the side of the bed to move the top half of the bed up or down as needed, depending on where the pain was worse on a particular day. So basically, I did the things that anyone could do. I didn't feel especially competent or helpful, but I hoped that my mere presence and willingness to help was beneficial for Maria in some way.

Monday, January 4

Maria's heartbeat seemed to be up and down a bit during the morning, so they tested her, and, fortunately, the results were normal.

Later, an attending neurologist came in with four or five residents, and she performed a brief physical exam, essentially the same exam that every neurologist who had looked at Maria had used to see how she was doing. Typically, these doctors pulled out their flashlights, and they looked in Maria's eyes. As they did so, they checked the movement of her eyes by asking her to look at a point directly in front of her and, then, gradually look to the left and to the right without moving her head. Initially, Maria struggled with this exercise, and she always moved her head to the side also, but now, she seemed to do it correctly. The doctors also asked Maria to squeeze the examining doctor's hand to physically gauge her strength, and, then, they performed a similar test where the doctors pushed down on Maria's ankles, one at a time, and they asked Maria to push up against the doctor's pressure to gauge the strength in her legs. Apparently, she was doing okay in these tests because they never mentioned a problem.

That afternoon, the speech specialist visited again. She observed Maria's swallowing, and she noticed that Maria's ability to swallow was not as strong as it was just days earlier, so she wanted to perform a special test the next day to actually measure that ability. She planned to do so by, first, having Maria swallow some barium, and, then, they would use a special machine to watch the barium go down and also watch as Maria attempted to swallow other foods and liquids.

Around 5:00 p.m., we received some good news. A physician assistant from the hematology department came to see Maria with an early but official report that Maria's lymph nodes did not show any indication of cancer. What a relief.

My sister Jenny and Maria's pastor, Pastor Duke, visited today, and Maria seemed to enjoy seeing them and talking to them. I think it helped her somehow to tell others, especially non-medical people, what she had experienced and what she was currently feeling at the time of their visits. Since Jenny and Pastor Duke knew and loved Maria, their reactions to her story and her circumstances were much more sympathetic than the medical people, and having the opportunity to share also seemed to take Maria's mind off her pain, for a short while at least.

Up to this point, Maria hadn't had a lot of visitors outside of family, partially because we didn't want to overwhelm Maria in the midst of her suffering and partially because of a surprise visit she received days earlier from some co-workers. These two young gentlemen showed up unannounced and were excited and enthusiastic, eager to let her know that they missed her and hoped that she would get better soon and return to work. That would have been a welcome visit if Maria had a broken bone that needed to heal or a simple surgical procedure that required a short hospital stay. In Maria's case, though, we still didn't know the problem or the long-range forecast for her release from the hospital. On top of that, Maria felt a bit embarrassed because, quite honestly, she didn't look that great when her co-workers arrived. She hadn't bathed yet that day, her hair was a mess, she had lost some weight on her normally thin frame, and she was in an ugly hospital gown. It's no wonder she felt uncomfortable, and, as a result, she asked us to screen all of her future visitors. Yes, she would be willing to see family and close friends but not people she did not know as well, and she definitely didn't want to see anyone if she were having a particularly difficult day either physically or emotionally.

Tuesday, January 5

On this day at about 9:45, the speech therapist visited Maria in preparation for the barium test. First, she brushed Maria's teeth, and, then, she let Maria know that a medical transport person would arrive in about an hour to bring her down to the basement for the test. And sure enough, at exactly 10:45, we began the journey downstairs from the fifth floor.

The therapist had told me earlier that I could accompany Maria, so I did so, and we entered a special room where all the equipment was set up. Maria was strapped into a special chair, so she could sit up for the procedure, and they put me in a small enclosure about ten feet away, so I could watch the test on a small monitor. It was like looking at an x-ray of Maria's head and torso, and I could see as the barium didn't quite go down because of Maria's difficulty in swallowing.

The therapist asked Maria to cough and swallow, and that only helped a little. Next, she fed Maria a bit of apple sauce to see if that would help the barium move down her throat, but that didn't quite work either. As a result, the therapist stopped the test at that point and didn't even continue with other foods. Instead, she recommended that Maria be fed, at least temporarily, through a tube in her nose down to her stomach because if Maria continued to struggle with swallowing, then food or liquid could accidentally go down into her lungs which would create an even more serious problem.

As I thought about Maria having to use a feeding tube, I had mixed emotions. One part of me was somewhat relieved because her three daily meal times had become quite stressful. She struggled to eat and drink, and I was worried that she would cough or choke on her food. I was also concerned that she was not getting enough nourishment because she had not been eating enough. Maria had always been thin, and she seemed to be getting even thinner and more frail during this hospital stay. So perhaps the feeding tube would allow her to get the nourishment and nutrition she needed to get stronger, so she could, gradually, return to actually eating solid foods, and, eventually, go home soon. That was a good thing.

Another part of me, however, had begun to worry that Maria's situation might not get better, and the swallowing problem might be just another sign of a more serious issue. Poor Maria still couldn't see clearly out of her right eye, and though I thought I heard a medical person say the sight in that eye would return to normal, that hadn't yet happened. Also, the speech therapist indicated that the feeding tube would be temporary, but what if that were not the case?

Fortunately, I tried not to let those negative thoughts stay with me too long because I could get too choked up if I thought about losing Maria, and I had to remain positive and optimistic. I simply kept praying for God to intervene.

"Dear Lord, please hold on to Your little girl. Please help her to recover, and please help me to stay strong and upbeat for her."

Just a clear diagnosis at that point would have been preferable to the continued uncertainty, even if the diagnosis involved a long and arduous road to recovery. The pessimistic part of me saw Maria sliding in one direction, and I was praying for a halt and a reversal. Any sign of progress at that point would have been so welcome.

Wednesday, January 6

Other than the placement of the feeding tube for Maria, this day was mostly uneventful. One doctor from cardiology visited as did one from neurology. A technician also performed an EKG on Maria, which I believe was the seventh such test they had performed in the 13 days that she had been in the hospital. Most of those results indicated that Maria had an irregular heartbeat, and in her case, it was unusually slow. When I was admitted back in early December, my heartbeat was unusually fast, and the doctors felt it was temporary due to stress. In Maria's case, they hadn't yet pinpointed the cause of the slow heartbeat, but, ironically, four of the seven EKGs indicated that the rate was abnormally slow, but three indicated that the rate was normal.

So was an uneventful day at that point a good day or a bad day? An optimist might say that "uneventful" is good and cite the cliché that "no news is good news." In other words, Maria's condition could have been considered stable, and after some of her early, tense days in the hospital, perhaps we should have been grateful.

However, a pessimist might say that "uneventful" is not good because Maria was still actually in the hospital and, apparently, not getting better, not making progress. A pessimist might say that the longer a person stays in the hospital, the less likely that person is to return home in a healthy condition.

What did I believe? As I have indicated earlier, by nature, I am an optimist, so I wanted to believe that an uneventful day was a good sign, just another indication that Maria's return to health might be a long road, but one that would eventually bring her home. That was what I sincerely wanted to believe. Honestly, though, I had to admit that the pessimistic thoughts were beginning to creep into my consciousness.

Fortunately, my optimistic thoughts returned near the end of the day when a surgeon who had been studying Maria's case visited. He said he would like to perform a laminectomy on Maria the following day to try and determine what was causing her back pain and her overall discomfort. He explained that this procedure was also known as decompression surgery, an attempt to create space in the spinal canal by removing the lamina — the back part of the vertebra that covers the spinal canal. The hope was that by enlarging the space in the spinal canal, that added space would relieve the pressure on Maria's spinal cord or nerves.

In addition, the surgeon said that since Maria's previous MRI showed an apparent liquid sac, he would attempt to remove that sac and later conduct a biopsy on the fluid in the sac.

Finally, he said he would also try to insert a lumbar drain, so that instead of a third lumbar puncture, the drain would easily eliminate any excess fluid from her spine which might relieve some of the pressure she was feeling.

Even though this surgeon was not guaranteeing that these actions would completely eliminate Maria's suffering and put her on a clear road to recovery, he explained that by performing those actions, he might improve her situation and, perhaps, in the process discover the real problem. We all agreed that the procedure was worth trying.

Thursday, January 7

On this day, a transport specialist visited Maria at about 10:00 to bring her downstairs for surgery later that morning. I accompanied Maria, and once we were in the pre-operating room, an anesthesiologist and the surgeon visited to explain what was about to happen. We both listened attentively, and I tried to take notes, so I could explain the process later to Barbara and Katrina if needed. Most of what the anesthesiologist and the surgeon said had been explained the previous day, but this time, the surgeon also mentioned the specific risks of this particular surgery.

The list of risks was frightening. Some terms he used I had never heard before, but the ones I understood hit me hard: bleeding, infection, paralysis, stroke, and death. I tried to remain calm as I looked at Maria, but she appeared unfazed, as if she were willing to try anything to get better. I prayed as I silently digested the possibilities, and I tried to convince myself that this warning was much like the list of possible side effects that they enumerate on television after a commercial for a particular medicine. Yes, anything is possible, but the warning is . . . well, just that — a warning. We had come to that point, we trusted this surgeon, and we had faith that he and God would pull Maria through this surgery.

And they did.

Around 1:00, the surgeon reported that the procedure went well. He performed the three tasks he had outlined earlier — the laminectomy, the draining of the liquid sac, and the insertion of the lumbar drain — and he said Maria tolerated the entire procedure satisfactorily with no complications.

He also explained that as part of the laminectomy, he removed some bone and epidural tissue which would be sent to the lab for analysis. Thus, he would have even more information for us the next day.

Naturally, Barbara and I had prayed all during the surgery, and, later, we offered prayers of thanksgiving as Maria rested after her ordeal and was later returned to her room. She seemed to be more comfortable than previously, and we assumed that the comfort was a result of both the drugs she had received for surgery and the fact that we were finally moving forward a bit, even if we didn't yet have any certainty about her condition.

Friday, January 8

The day after Maria's initial surgery, a physical therapist visited in the afternoon to try and get Maria up and moving somewhat. Though she looked weak, Maria did move from the bed to a nearby reclining chair and also did a few exercises with the therapist while still sitting in the chair. Maria also managed to sit upright in the chair for a short while before she asked that the chair be reclined a bit more, so she could sleep. By 5:00, she was resting comfortably.

Regarding the results from the previous day, the surgeon said he would like to operate on Maria again on the following Monday, so he could insert a shunt which would act as a more permanent drain and make it even easier to remove any excess fluid. In addition, he said he would like to do a biopsy of a lymph node in Maria's neck.

And speaking of biopsies and other tests, the result of the spinal cord biopsy was benign, and another test for myeloma — a cancer that arises in plasma cells, a type of white blood cell — came back negative. Naturally, those results gave us some hope, but still no definite diagnosis; plus, Maria would soon face another surgery. All we could do in the meantime was keep on praying.

Saturday, January 9

We expected a quiet weekend before Maria's follow-up surgery on Monday, and that was pretty much what we got. The only medical information we dealt with was a chest exam to rule out pneumonia. Once again, fortunately, the results were good. According to the doctor, Maria's lungs were "clear and normally inflated."

Maria seemed to be feeling a bit stronger too and in better spirits. She felt so good, in fact, that she posted a personal update on Facebook, her first post in almost two weeks:

> My 30th birthday started with a bang by experiencing my first migraine. Then on

Christmas, I was rushed to the hospital by ambulance for blurred vision and confusion. Since being in the hospital, I've had a successful back surgery which relieved a lot of the pain. And on Monday, I'll have a shunt placed in my head to release any additional liquid. Prayers appreciated. My doctors, my support system, my family, and all the prayer support is greatly appreciated.

I was so touched by Maria's post that I decided that I, too, needed to thank some people. So as she rested after posting her message, I pulled out my pen and notebook and composed the following, which I shared on the employee bulletin board. (I also used a portion of this note in the dedication of this book.)

> To Everyone Working on the Neurology Floor:
> Thank you. You have been taking care of my daughter Maria for over two weeks now. She was admitted on Christmas Day, and during that time, she has been in three different rooms with a wide variety of people helping her. Every single one of you is phenomenal.
> From the attending physicians and specialists to the resident doctors, from the registered nurses to the patient care assistants, and from those who deliver the food, to those who clean the patients' rooms and hallways, and anyone I may have missed, thank you.
> You have all been patient and kind, understanding and compassionate, and sweet and generous. Your professional abilities and

talents are superb, but your human tenderness is beyond belief and well beyond the call of duty.

For example, when Maria was feeling weak after her admission and had questions about her diet, one of you recommended a protein bar that would help her when she didn't have time to eat a full meal; then, you disappeared and returned a few minutes later with a sample bar from your personal locker, so Maria could eat it when needed.

A week later when Maria couldn't sleep one night and needed a diversion, one of you purchased a deck of cards and some artistic supplies, so she could use them to take her mind off her pain.

Finally, as Maria's mom and sister and I spent countless hours by Maria's bedside, you all offered to help make us comfortable as well. You brought us coffee and water, you microwaved food for us, and you treated us all with respect and patience at all times, even when we were peppering you with too many questions at inconvenient times.

Once again, we say thank you — a million times thank you. We could not have asked for better care for our daughter, and we are forever grateful to all of you. You are truly God's angels doing God's work.

Sunday, January 10

We usually go to church on Sunday, yet none of us had been to a Sunday service since Maria was admitted on Christmas Day. So we were pleasantly surprised when a hospital chaplain, who also served as a minister at a nearby Christian church, visited Maria for a short time this morning. He chatted with her for a bit, gave her some written materials, and at her request, he read to her from the Bible, from chapter four of Paul's letter to the Philippians.

Initially, I wasn't sure why she chose that particular chapter, but as the chaplain read it aloud, several verses stood out, some of which Maria had probably memorized in her youth. Though Maria wasn't talking a lot at this point, I'm guessing she drew some strength from these verses:

> Verses 6 and 7 — "Do not be anxious about anything, but in everything, by prayer and petition, with thanksgiving, present your requests to God. And the peace of God, which transcends all understanding, will guard your hearts and your minds in Christ Jesus."

> Verse 8 — "Finally, brothers and sisters, whatever is true, whatever is noble, whatever is right, whatever is pure, whatever is lovely, whatever is admirable — if anything is excellent or praiseworthy — think about such things."

Verses 12 and 13 — "I know what it is to be in need, and I know what it is to have plenty. I have learned the secret of being content in any and every situation, whether well fed or hungry, whether living in plenty or in want. I can do everything through him who gives me strength."

Verse 20 — "To our God and Father, be glory for ever and ever. Amen." (New International Version)

Later that afternoon, a resident visited and adjusted Maria's headache medicine to try and relieve some of her pain. She also checked a rash that had developed on Maria's chest. The resident felt the rash was a reaction to one of Maria's antibiotics, so she recommended that Maria simply take Benadryl instead which might cause Maria to become sleepy. That sounded like a good side effect to me since Maria had trouble sleeping in the hospital since her arrival.

Finally, a resident who would be present at Maria's surgery the next day came in and asked if Maria had any questions about the surgery. Not surprisingly, she did have a few.

- What is the shunt made of? (Synthetic plastic.)
- Will the lumbar drain be removed? (Yes.)
- Do I still have staples in my back from the previous surgery, and, if so, what are they made of? (Yes. The staples are metal, but they will be removed in the near future.)
- Will they have to shave my head? If so, where and how much? (Yes. Just above the ear on the right side and only about a quarter of an inch.)

- How long will the surgery take? (The surgery itself will only take one hour, but the entire procedure, including preparation beforehand and recovery afterwards, will take about four hours.)

Monday, January 11

The same surgeon who operated on Maria during the previous week was scheduled to operate on her again. Thus, we again met with the anesthesiologist and the surgeon beforehand, and, again, they warned us of the same risks mentioned previously: bleeding, infection, paralysis, stroke, and death, among others.

In this case, though, the surgeon mentioned that he felt Maria's problem might be a condition called hydrocephalus which occurs when there is excess fluid accumulating in the brain. Laymen sometimes refer to this as "water on the brain," but it's not water; it's cerebrospinal fluid (CSF). This excess fluid can add pressure to the brain and cause damage. To prevent that damage from occurring, the surgeon wanted to place a shunt (basically, a drainage tube) to allow that fluid to be redirected and removed, and he also wanted to remove the lumbar drainage catheter which they had been using earlier for a similar purpose. Finally, he wanted to explore and remove some lymph nodes in Maria's neck area, so they could be examined as well.

Afterwards, while Maria was still in recovery, the surgeon reported that everything went smoothly. The shunt had been inserted, and the lumbar drain catheter had been removed. He also extracted samples of the lymph nodes for examination. He felt that the shunt would reduce the pressure on Maria's brain and ease her headache pain, but he didn't yet have a clear diagnosis of the overall problem. He did indicate that the results of the biopsy of the lymph nodes would provide more answers to our questions.

Fortunately, during the afternoon after the surgery, Maria did seem to be sleeping more peacefully, and as Barbara and I drove home that night, we both felt a bit more optimistic that the medical people were coming closer and closer to a diagnosis, one that we assumed would eventually allow us to bring Maria home to begin her recovery.

Tuesday, January 12

This day simply felt like a waiting day since the medical professionals were evaluating the results of the prior day's surgery and the analysis of Maria's lymph nodes. Doctors from neurology, radiology, and oncology visited Maria, and according to them, everything looked normal except for some blood cells which looked abnormal. As one of the doctors said before leaving Maria's room, "We are still trying to piece it together."

By this point, quite honestly, Maria seemed to be fading a bit. She was still in some pain and struggling, but she wasn't as verbal about her suffering. She was quiet for longer periods of time, and even when we tried to engage her in conversation, she seemed uninterested or too weak to say much.

She also stated again that she did not want to see anyone outside the family. Some of her close friends and some acquaintances from church came to the hospital, but when we explained the situation, they were all very respectful and understanding. Rather than leave immediately, though, many of them gathered in a big waiting room down at the end of the hall. There, we were able to interact with them, and many of them gathered in small groups to pray for Maria and for us. That was encouraging, of course, but when we returned to Maria's room, the reality of her situation hit us again, and we found ourselves praying even more.

Wednesday, January 13

Looking back at this day, I realized that this was the beginning of the end. For most of Maria's time in the hospital, we were waiting for a diagnosis, one that would lead to a clear path of treatment and recovery. On this day, we began to receive some early indicators regarding her diagnosis, but these indicators were not good.

A breast exam, for example, showed a hardened mass, and the doctors were worried that this might be breast cancer and that it might have spread to Maria's brain. I was not present when the oncologist met with Barbara and Katrina, but he said if that were the case, the prognosis would be "poor."

He added that he wanted to consult further with a breast cancer specialist for a more definitive diagnosis, and he also emphasized that at that point, Maria would still have some treatment options.

Later, as Barbara and Katrina tried to explain to Maria what the doctor had said, despite her struggles to communicate, she seemed to understand the key point, and she said something that broke my heart when they told me later. She said, "I'm too young to die."

Thursday, January 14

After another long day of waiting, at around eight o'clock, in that big visitor lounge just down the hall from Maria's room, Barbara, Katrina, and I met with a breast cancer specialist. At that hour, the room was mostly deserted, and we sat at a round table in a far corner away from the door. There, he told us that based on all the information from all the tests and the surgeries, it looked like Maria had a type of cancer called lobular breast carcinoma with leptomeningeal spread. Basically, that meant that, as feared, Maria did have a previously undetected breast cancer that had, indeed, spread to her brain. And, unfortunately, the prognosis was not good. He was completely honest with us and concluded that he felt that Maria might only have two to three months to live.

That news, needless to say, was overwhelming. We were all stunned — and silent for a bit. As the doctor spoke, I know I tried to maintain my composure and stay strong for Barbara and Katrina. I also asked what I thought were the appropriate questions about the cancer and how it had spread. When Katrina finally asked about possible treatments, he said no good ones existed. Two or three methods were possible, but they might only extend Maria's life by a few months, and they would all involve invasive procedures, difficult side effects, and long hospital stays. He gently suggested we should begin to think about Hospice care for Maria.

When the doctor left us, we all broke down. In fact, I think we all pretty much cried all night. Yes, we composed ourselves when we returned to Maria's room where she was sleeping. We sat with her for a while, silently. We were all absorbing the news and trying to make sense of it all. Later, with Maria still sleeping, we said, "Good night" to her before we left. Then, we maintained a stoic front as we exited the wing, took the elevator to the main floor, and walked down the long corridor to the parking lot and our cars. As we walked, Barbara suggested to Katrina that instead of going to her apartment alone, she might want to spend the night with us, and she agreed. Once in the car, however, the three of us were alone with the news that we were going to lose our daughter and our sister.

When we arrived home a half hour later, it was pretty late, and we were all pretty exhausted, but we did not sleep immediately or easily. We took turns crying and comforting one another in the living room. And when we all finally went to bed, we slept fitfully.

At one point, I got out of bed to kneel and pray. Kneeling in prayer next to a bed is the picture we all have in our minds for prayer, but I rarely pray in that position. Usually, at night, I simply lie in bed and relive the day in my mind, and if I am not too exhausted, I thank God for the blessings that he gave me that day, I ask Him to forgive me for the mistakes I made that day, I ask Him to help me with my plans for the next day, and I praise Him for His provision and His faithfulness. If Barbara is with me and awake, we pray together. Only when I am in desperate need of help, however, do I kneel down next to the bed. Obviously, I knelt on this night.

Then, before I even uttered a word to God, Barbara got up and knelt down next to me on my side of the bed. Honestly, I don't recall the exact words we prayed that night, but I believe they were something like this:

First, we asked God for a healing miracle for Maria. We asked that she be restored to complete health immediately, so that she could return to work and, especially, to her graduate classes for teaching, a goal she so deeply desired.

But we also asked God for strength and wisdom and patience and understanding just in case God did not have a healing miracle in mind for Maria. Basically, we came back to the Lord's prayer. Yes, we desperately and selfishly wanted our Maria to get better, to return to health, to walk out of that hospital on her own, and continue her life here on Earth. Yet, we were also totally committed to our God and to His will and to

His plan for us. If He were ready to take Maria home soon for some reason, we would accept that situation as well as we could. "Your will be done" (Matthew 6:10) was the one specific phrase I remember from my prayer that night, a phrase that confirms our total submission to God's will and a phrase that is so similar to what Jesus Himself said to God the Father in the Garden of Gethsamene the night before Jesus was crucified on the cross: "My Father, if it is not possible for this cup to be taken away unless I drink it, may Your will be done" (Matthew 26:42).

Looking back at that time, I know some people might say that our prayer was "double minded." On one hand, we were asking for a miracle, but at the same time, we were resigning ourselves to the fact that our God might not give us a miracle. In fact, I have heard some preachers say that if we firmly believe and if we have total faith in God, then He will answer our prayers, but if we waver at all, or if we don't fully believe, then He will not answer our prayers.

I struggle with that idea because I feel like it places too much of the responsibility for the miracle on us as humans and too little of the responsibility on God. Obviously, only God can perform miracles, and, obviously, God has a master plan for us, so if He were ready to bring our Maria home, despite our prayers and our desires, who were we to question His plan? His will for our family? Yes, I love my Maria, and I wanted her with us, yet I also love God, and I trusted Him fully with my life and with Maria's life. So I keep going back to that phrase, "Not my will, but Yours be done" (Luke 22:42).

Friday, January 15

We returned to the hospital before 10:00 because the doctor we met with on Thursday night said we should all visit Maria together to try to explain what was happening to her.

Unfortunately, Maria was not awake enough or coherent enough to converse at that time. So the doctor simply checked her vital signs, and he told us that we could meet later in the day with another doctor who had a better idea of what Maria was going through.

When we met with that second doctor for a second opinion, he indicated that Maria might not even have the two or three months mentioned by the previous doctor. Instead, he said that Maria might only have four weeks. As he explained Maria's condition, he said that the cancer in Maria's brain was not a single mass that could potentially be removed through surgery; her cancer was more like a collection of snowflakes that had fallen into her brain, and it would be impossible to remove all of them and still save Maria.

With that in mind, this doctor also indicated we could only try to keep Maria comfortable, and that we might want to think about Hospice care for her. That second use of the word "Hospice" by that second doctor hit me hard because our family had used Hospice for my dad's last week of life before he died at the age of 89 from pancreatic cancer. He had become extremely weak, and he was sleeping almost all of the time. Fortunately, in Dad's case, he was still living at home, and he was able to remain there and to pass in his own bed surrounded by family members about a week after the Hospice care had begun.

Maria's case was a bit different. The medical staff didn't feel that we could adequately take care of Maria at home because she was suffering so much and needed the medical people to provide the drugs or treatments that would relieve or eliminate her pain. As a result, they recommended that she be transferred to the Hospice wing at another hospital nearby.

Before we made that decision, though, we wanted to talk to Maria about the news we had received. How do you tell your daughter that she's dying? Both doctors had graciously agreed to be with us, so we could all be there together to break the news and answer any questions she might have. In both cases, though, on Thursday night and Friday morning, Maria was not coherent enough for us to speak to her. Her need for rest and her pain medications kept her somewhat out of it, and quite honestly, we sometimes preferred that state for her because when she was awake and alert, she was either mildly uncomfortable or in pain.

As Maria's dad, I was uncertain about the prospect of explaining the situation to her. On one hand, I wanted a doctor there with us to describe what was going on since I didn't feel comfortable with all the medical terms. I also didn't want Katrina to have to do it. Yes, as a physician assistant, I was sure she could have explained it all, but I didn't want her to bear that responsibility of explaining that terrible news to her only sister.

At the same time, I wasn't sure I could be strong enough to speak that news to Maria. I again recalled Maria's high-school graduation party at our home, and during the prayer before we ate, I tried to give thanks not only for the food and for Maria's accomplishment but also for all the joy that she had brought to us during her first 18 years of life. I could not get through what I wanted to say. I thanked God for the food and for Maria's graduation, but then I broke down. I couldn't finish. So if I broke down on a happy and joyous occasion, how would I be able to remain strong and composed to tell my daughter that she was going to leave us to join Jesus in heaven?

Also, I worried about how Maria would react to the news. One part of me expected her to react like the strong Christian woman that she was and to quickly say something simple and straightforward like, "If that is God's will for me and for my life, then I will graciously accept what He has for me."

Another part of me, though, expected to see the defiant and strong and stubborn Maria who might say, "No, I'm not going to die. I'm going to fight and resist and persevere. I'm going to beat this, so I can get back to work and to my graduate studies in education to become a teacher."

And a final part of me expected her to be initially scared and overwhelmed by the news just as we were when we first heard it. She might break down in tears, she might be totally shocked and unable to comprehend it all, or her brain may have already been so affected that she might not even understand what we were saying or what it meant to her. The whole situation was so hard to digest, and I didn't know what to say or do or how to react to what was going on. And how would I say good-bye to my daughter when the time came? This wasn't like leaving our baby in the children's nursery at church for the first time. In that case, I think Barbara stayed with her for the first 15 minutes to make sure Maria was comfortable there. And this wasn't like leaving the three-year-old Maria at nursery school for her first day because Barbara would return for her two and a half hours later. This wasn't even like any of the other major adventures of her life — her first sleepover, her first weekend at a youth conference, her first week-long missions trip, or her first college semester at a school which was five hours away from home.

No, this good-bye would actually be harder on us than on her because we would be left behind. On this particular journey, she might be afraid, but she would close her eyes one final time, and then she would wake up in heaven for eternity. Barbara and Katrina and I, though, would be left behind without her for who knows how long before we would be reunited with her in heaven. We would be the ones who would want Maria to remain 15 minutes longer, so we could try to get comfortable with the situation. We would be the nervous ones wondering if we could get through the morning, through the evening, through the weekend, and through the week and the semester ahead and, then, through the unknown years beyond.

Oh, Maria, how will we go on without you?

Saturday, January 16

On this day, I called all four of my sisters to tell them about the four-week diagnosis for Maria. Up to that point, I had been relaying some of the medical information through Jenny just to save myself from having to make four phone calls every time we got a new piece of news. Jenny lives nearby and had visited Maria a few times here at the hospital, and she was more than willing to pass along the information to Kathy, Marie, and Anne.

This information, however, was different. Though I knew it would be difficult to say the words to them, I didn't want my sisters to hear it from anyone else. So at some point around lunch time, when Barbara and Katrina were present with Maria, I went to find an isolated space where I could make the calls. I knew I'd be crying as I spoke, and I wanted some privacy.

Initially, I went to the hospital chapel on the first floor, but some people were already sitting there, apparently waiting for a service or a prayer group to begin. Next, I found what I thought would be a quiet spot near one of the bridges to the parking garage. I called Kathy, my older sister, first, but she wasn't home, so I called my younger sisters next.

"Marie, it's Jim," I said. Marie, too, had come to the hospital to visit Maria, so she asked how Maria was doing. I could barely speak without breaking down completely, but somehow, I choked out the words, "It's bad news." Again I paused, trying to contain my emotions and trying to find the right words. Marie waited. I'm sure she could sense my difficulty.

"Take your time," she said to put me at ease.

"Four weeks," I said. "The doctors are only giving Maria four weeks." We both cried at that point.

"Jim. I'm so sorry."

Unfortunately at that moment, some people walked through what I thought was my isolated spot, and I didn't hear everything else Marie said. I'm sure she said she was sorry again, and I'm pretty sure she offered to do anything we needed. I know she also offered to call my other sisters, but I told her I wanted to do it myself. When we finished speaking, I wiped my tears, blew my nose, and knew I had to find a better spot for the remaining three calls.

So I took the elevator back up to the fifth floor to the large waiting room down the hall from where Maria received her care, the same room where the first doctor had given us the initial bad news two nights earlier. That room, too, was occupied, though, so I turned the corner near the elevators in the opposite direction and found a quiet corner between the area where two adjacent buildings come together. No one was in the vicinity, so I literally buried my face in the corner and made three more calls. They did not get any easier.

Each time, I started my explanation with those tragic words: "It's bad news." As I thought about the experience later, these words were similar to what my dad would say to me whenever he had to call to tell me about the passing of an older relative.

"Jim, it's Dad. I have some bad news."

Subconsciously, I guess I was modeling what Dad had taught me to do in this type of situation.

My sisters' reactions were all similar to Marie's reaction: shock, disbelief, tears, and a struggle to find words. Honestly, I can't recall their specific words, but

I do remember Anne saying simply and sympathetically, "Oh, Jim!"

Since Jenny and Marie lived nearby, they both said they would come to see us soon, and Anne and Kathy, who lived four and five hours away, said they could come the following weekend. Ironically, everyone on my side of the family was already planning on being in the area on Saturday the 23rd because my niece, Renee (Jenny's oldest child and Maria's cousin) was also about to turn 30, and her husband, Greg, had arranged for a surprise party.

As I thought about what was happening to Maria, I somehow knew and felt that she would not leave us immediately. I knew, or I believed at that time, that she would still be with us the following weekend when other family members also came into town for the party. I had heard many stories of people who were dying and how they waited to pass until another family member had arrived. In fact, we experienced it about a year and a half earlier when my father passed away.

We were at his house on a Saturday afternoon, and he had already been placed under Hospice care. He was not doing well that day, and only my sister Anne was not present. She was planning to come the following Monday, but I called her and told her she should come as soon as possible. She immediately changed her weekend plans and hopped in the car. Four hours later she arrived, and she was able to see Dad one last time and spend some time with him before he passed later that night.

Obviously, I didn't know how long Maria would live, but I simply had the feeling that she would hold on at least until after Renee's party. In fact, about a week or so earlier, Renee's sister, Kyla, visited Maria, and they talked about the party. Kyla raised the idea of postponing the party for Maria's sake, but Maria said she didn't want them to do that; Maria wanted Renee to be celebrated, even if Maria herself probably wouldn't be able to attend.

Sunday, January 17

By this point, Maria was no longer able to communicate with us, and she had not previously filled out a living will for herself or a medical power of attorney. Thus, as her parents, Barbara and I were legally bound to make medical decisions for her. Naturally, we also consulted with Katrina and with the doctors who had been advising us. After much thought and prayer, we collectively decided that Hospice care was the best option for our Maria, and once we communicated that decision to the medical staff, they began the process of transferring Maria to that other hospital which offered the palliative care we desired for her. That process included two more decisions that I had not anticipated: one involving the Do Not Resuscitate (DNR) form and one that involved removing Maria's feeding tube.

The DNR form was needed, so that if Maria had another seizure or some other type of medical emergency, the doctors would not take extraordinary means to keep her alive. The main goal at that point was to keep Maria comfortable and out of pain. We had watched her suffer in that hospital bed for almost a month, and nothing positive was happening, and the doctors were not offering any reasonable treatment options. We needed to prepare to say good-bye.

Personally, we were familiar with the DNR form because my dad had signed one for himself at some point during the last year of his life. In fact, his medical advisors suggested that he not only tell all of his family members about the form, but they also suggested that he post the signed, bright pink form right inside his front door, so that it would be visible to all who entered the house. In that way, if any medical people entered the home due to an emergency call, they would know and understand the situation and provide Dad with comfort care rather than attempt to provide recovery care.

Since my dad was approaching age 90 when he signed his form, I was saddened, but I understood his decision. In fact, he made his decision easily because he had witnessed a situation where a DNR would have been preferable to what actually happened.

Before my Uncle John passed away, he had a heart attack while cutting his lawn, and his sister Mary called an ambulance, and she also called my dad who lived just blocks away. Both my dad and the ambulance arrived at about the same time, so my dad witnessed everything as the paramedics tried to bring his older brother back to life.

As Dad told me about it later, I could tell he was deeply affected by the experience: "It was obvious that John was dead," he told me, "but they kept pounding on his chest to try to bring him back to life. I wanted them to stop, but I didn't say anything. When they finally gave up and pronounced him dead, I realized I never want anyone to do that to me. When it's time for me to go, I just want to go. I don't want medical people trying to save me at all costs, and I definitely don't want to be hooked up to machines in a hospital."

As he told me the story, I was reminded of the poem "Do Not Go Gentle into That Good Night" by Welsh poet Dylan Thomas (1914-1953). In the poem, the speaker tries to encourage his dying father to fight and try to hold on to life. The son says, "Rage, rage against the dying of the light. Do not go gentle into that good night."

As a young man, when I read that poem to my students, I could identify with the son's passion. I could relate to the idea that life is priceless and should be cherished and preserved at all costs. As I became older, however, and witnessed my dad's deterioration and suffering from pancreatic cancer, I could also identify with his resignation and his willingness to leave when he felt his time had come.

In Maria's case, at age 30, she was much too young to die, but she had also suffered and lost too much, and the doctors had nothing to offer her. So just as my dad did not want the medical personnel to pound away at his brother's heart, I did not want to prolong Maria's suffering, especially if they did not hold out any hope for her survival.

So, yes, we signed the Do Not Resuscitate form for our daughter, but we did so with the belief that she was not merely leaving this world; instead, she was entering into heaven where she would be reunited not only with my dad who had predeceased her by a year and a half but also with Jesus Christ, the God who had created her, died on the cross for her, and came back to life for her. When her time here on Earth ended, He would be the one to welcome her into His loving arms in heaven.

While the DNR decision was difficult, it did make sense to me. The decision to remove Maria's feeding tube, however, stunned me. I guess I assumed that they would continue to feed Maria and nourish her as the cancer gradually took her away from us. Removing the feeding tube seemed like we were hastening the process, and I think I felt somewhat guilty, as if I were actually killing her rather than letting the cancer take her away.

As we talked about it, though, Katrina explained it in a way that was logical and made sense and also put me at ease and alleviated the guilt I was feeling. She explained that as long as they kept feeding Maria, Maria would still continue to suffer from the cancer because her body was still trying to survive. Once they removed the feeding tube, however, the medical people could focus solely on keeping Maria comfortable and pain free. Essentially, they would be allowing Maria to go peacefully, just as we had hoped when we made the Hospice decision rather than make her struggle to finish a journey that was about to end in either case. And after watching Maria suffer for almost a month already, I knew I didn't want to watch her struggle any longer.

As I wrote that last sentence, I began to think about other families who had lost loved ones and who had watched those loved ones suffer for much more than a month — years, in fact. Understandably, those people might say that we were fortunate by comparison. That comparison makes sense logically, of course, but emotionally and spiritually, it didn't help us in any way. We were devastated by all that we were going through.

Monday, January 18

This was Maria's last full day in the hospital before they transferred her to the Hospice facility. She was no longer fully coherent, so we tried to explain to her that she would be moved to another facility where they would try to ease her pain and make her more comfortable. At that point, she did express her desire to go home, but we also explained that we wouldn't be able to give her the care she needed. I'm not sure if she fully comprehended what we told her. She seemed to accept our explanation, and soon afterwards, she again drifted off to sleep.

At that point, we had spent almost a month at the hospital, and for a fair amount of time, we greeted visitors and sat in the big waiting room outside the neuroscience wing. This room is at the end of one hallway and just around the corner from the elevators. The room is approximately the size of a classroom that could seat 30 to 40 students with a small television on the wall at each end and a big soda machine in the middle. Chairs and couches fill the wall opposite the televisions. Since Maria's room could only hold a few visitors at a time, we often retreated to this waiting area when too many visitors were present or when Maria was sleeping or wanted some private time with family members or close friends.

During one of our final days there, I noticed a married couple who were in a somewhat similar situation, and through some minor conversation with the dad, I learned of their son's issues. The son was about 20 years old and in college, and he — like Maria — had some neurological issues. Unlike Maria, this young man had been suffering with these issues for a few years, but he had always overcome them, and his parents appeared confident that he would overcome this particular issue as well. Fortunately for this family, the son's issues had not been brought on by cancer. Thus, as Maria's situation quickly deteriorated because of the spreading cancer and we became more and more worried, this couple appeared, to us at least, somewhat relaxed and carefree — though I'm sure that was not the case. As I observed them talking to one another and to others on their phones, they seemed to indicate that their son would be leaving the hospital in the near future, and they would all go on with their ordinary lives. On this particular day, however, everything changed.

For whatever reason, their son's situation worsened, and they would not be leaving the hospital as soon as they had expected. As a result, their demeanor changed. Understandably, they appeared more nervous and concerned, and their tone of voice sounded worried and tentative. Naturally, I felt called to pray for them, and during a subsequent conversation with the dad, I asked if I could do so. He agreed easily and quickly, and I prayed for all of us: for Maria and for their son, for all the people who are treating and helping our children, and for us as parents that we would be there for our children and willingly do whatever was needed.

And in the midst of that prayer, I felt a certain freedom and a release. I knew our Maria was soon going home to Jesus, and I would never again have to worry or pray for any of her earthly problems. She would be transformed and made new and be reunited with her Creator in heaven for eternity. She would be delivered. Our role as her earthly parents would be completely and successfully fulfilled.

This boy's parents, though, would have to keep praying. They would remain worried and concerned until he once again recovered from or adjusted to his medical difficulties. Then, they would take him home, he would return to his college classes, and their earthly lives would continue.

Barbara, Katrina, and I would also go on with our earthly lives but without our Maria. So would I rather have Maria here with us? Selfishly, of course, I would. As her father, I wanted to see her fulfill her goals: to earn her master's degree in teaching, to have her own classroom and students, to fall in love, get married, and have children. Maria's medical situation reminded me so much of when Maria went off to college; in both cases, I couldn't hold her back. It's almost as if God had pulled up in His car in front of our house and said, "Hi, Jim. Are you ready for Maria to go off to the place I have prepared for her?"

Quite honestly, I was not completely ready to see Maria go off with her Creator, just as I was not completely ready to send Maria five hours away to college when she was 18. I struggled. I missed her. I thought about her and prayed for her often after she left. However, I knew and I believed that God had a plan for Maria's life and for our lives, and I trusted that this is what God wanted for Maria, so I released her to Him. I love Maria, and I love my Lord Jesus.

Tuesday, January 19

This was a long, tough day. It was the first day of the spring semester, so I needed to return to work and get a few things done in the morning, but I also wanted to be at the hospital because they were going to move Maria to Hospice care later in the afternoon.

So, first, I went to see my boss to explain to her what was going on and that I needed some time off. I struggled to speak, but I managed to explain the situation and that I would definitely need to take the rest of the day off and, most likely, the rest of the week and the following week.

Then, I repeated the same message to my co-worker who would be most affected by my absence, and to the head of the English department where I taught two classes in addition to my primary job in The Writing Center. All of them were extremely shocked because I hadn't been in touch with them since the end of the fall semester. Fortunately, they were all sympathetic and supportive, and all were more than willing to accommodate me in any way they could. In fact, the head of the English department offered to find replacements for me to teach my classes if I wanted to give them up, but I told her that holding on to them might be good for me under the circumstances.

In each case, too, I asked all three women to keep the information confidential because I wasn't yet ready to share Maria's story with everyone. Ironically, while I was holding back, Barbara and Katrina had agreed to let friends of Maria put a prayer request for her on Facebook:

> Our friend Maria is in the hospital and fighting for her life and needs a miracle. I'm asking everyone I know to pray for that miracle and to share this post to let her and her family know that we are standing with her and believing for that miracle. I'm asking everyone to share this post so we can get as many people around the world praying for her! Please join us.

When I heard about the Facebook message, I had to laugh at the irony, but I was somewhat relieved too. Trying to tell others was too draining, so a public post of the news made it a lot easier.

Around 4:00 o'clock that afternoon, the transport service came to bring Maria from the hospital to the Hospice facility. We had already cleaned out all the cards and gifts and miscellaneous stuff we had accumulated there, and two or three nurses and patient-care assistants were taking care of all of Maria's medical paraphernalia such as her IV drip and the devices that measured all of her vital signs.

Meanwhile, the transport workers had wheeled in their bed to move Maria from the hospital to the ambulance, and in the midst of all that craziness, one particularly kind and compassionate patient care associate noticed that Maria's feet were uncovered. And even though Maria was somewhat out of it at the time, this tender soul spoke to Maria sweetly and lovingly.

"Maria, it's cold out there today, definitely below freezing. I'm going to get you a pair of socks."

Then, this young woman left the room and returned within 30 seconds with a pair of those ugly, but warm, red-and-white socks with the slip-proof attachments on the bottom. She gently lifted Maria's feet, one at a time, and slowly and carefully rolled the socks over Maria's toes and ankles up to the mid-point of her calves. This compassionate servant would likely never see Maria again, and Maria was leaving to spend her final days on earth in another hospital, yet this young girl did not want Maria's feet to be cold on the two-mile ambulance journey from one hospital to the next. Of all the wonderful care that Maria had received during her extensive hospital stay, this simple Christ-like act of love and compassion was the sweetest instance of simple human kindness I have ever witnessed.

Once the medical people finished their work, they helped the transport staff move Maria from the hospital bed to the mobile ambulance bed. Then, the two ambulance workers covered Maria with warm, thick blankets, so that only her face would be exposed to the cold outside. Normally, family members are not allowed to ride in the back of the ambulance with the patient, but these two, young, kind servants said I could be there with Maria. I'm guessing they felt sorry for me because my daughter was being moved to a Hospice facility, and I definitely appreciated their kindness.

After the elevator ride downstairs, they wheeled Maria through the hallways in the basement to the exit and the waiting ambulance. I walked alongside Maria, and she appeared to be sleeping, quiet and motionless. She opened her eyes a bit when we hit the cold air outside, and they lifted her bed into the ambulance. Then, they let me climb in after her, and as I struggled to move in such tight quarters, I fell forward a bit and reached out my hands to catch myself, and my hands landed on Maria's thighs.

"Dad, what are you doing?" she said, somewhat annoyed that I had disturbed her rest.

"I'm sorry, Sweetheart," I apologized immediately, and though I was sorry and embarrassed for my minor loss of balance, I was also a bit excited by Maria's reaction. She still had some life left in her.

During the short ride, I looked at Maria, and I also looked out the back window, and I watched as people carried on with their daily, late-afternoon activities: walking home from work or school, shopping, exercising, walking their dogs. The scene reminded me of my first real experience with death over 50 years earlier.

I was only 12 years old when my four-year-old sister, Peggy, died. She had always had serious medical issues during her short life, but I never expected her to die. When she passed, I was so shocked and overwhelmed that when we drove down Main Street to her funeral on that spring morning, I couldn't believe that other people were simply going on with their lives as if nothing had happened. "Didn't they know that Peggy had died?" I wondered. "Shouldn't they be going to her funeral too?"

I felt pretty much the same way on this day. My little girl Maria was dying, yet these people didn't care. Our loss was so big and so all consuming, yet we were just a small wave in the great ocean of life. Maria's wave had come to shore and rested there for just over 30 years, and now she was returning to the sea.

When we arrived at the Hospice facility and as we made our way to the fifth floor, I was also reminded of an earlier visit I had made to that particular unit. The elderly father of one of our neighbors was dying, and his family had brought him to Hospice, so he could pass comfortably. I didn't know him well, but we had met four or five times over the years, usually at a picnic or at a birthday or graduation party, and we had always gotten along well and conversed easily. We both enjoyed those times together. So when our neighbor told me her dad was near the end, I wanted to see him and talk to him one more time. I assumed our final meeting would be a sad but pleasant farewell. I was wrong.

By the time I visited him, late on a Monday evening, his family had already gone home, and he, too, like Maria, was well on his way home to Jesus. He was alone, lying in his bed as if sleeping, but his breathing was slow and loud and strained, as if any one breath could be his last. I was startled and a little frightened I have to admit. At that time (which was prior to my own father's passing), I had never been that close to death before. I didn't know what to do, so I sat on the chair next to his bed and just watched him breathe for a while. I realized quickly that we would not have a final conversation, so I began to pray. I thanked God for his life, for the opportunity I had to get to know him, and I prayed for his entire family that they might find comfort in his passing and be grateful for his long life with them. I stayed with him for probably 30 minutes, and before I left, I told him how much I had enjoyed his company, and I told him that I looked forward to seeing him again in heaven. Quite honestly, I don't know if he could hear me, and I didn't know if he had a personal relationship with Jesus, but I encouraged him to talk to his Creator if possible, and then I said good night and good-bye.

That final experience with him all came back to me as they wheeled Maria into that beautiful but sad Hospice wing. I remembered the front desk and the nurses' station, and I recalled the eerie quietness of that particular wing. Our Maria, just like our neighbor's dad, had come there to die. We didn't know how much time she had left, but we knew she would never come home again.

Wednesday, January 20

The next day was much less hectic as we settled into Maria's new surroundings. As I sat with Maria in her room, I noticed a picture frame on the wall. The eight-by-ten-inch frame was filled with a cross stitch of the face of Jesus Christ. I was caught off guard because the walls at the previous hospital had no decorations whatsoever, so I was pleasantly surprised to see that the image of my Lord and Savior welcomed His daughter and my daughter to her final destination in this life. Gradually, I realized that the picture of Christ was present because we were in a Catholic facility, founded and maintained by people who believe, as I do, that Jesus Christ is our Creator and Provider, and the picture reminded me that He would be with us all in Maria's final days, however many she might have.

Once Maria was settled into her new room, I also realized that this particular wing of the hospital was different from the previous hospital in many other ways, and this is not to criticize the previous hospital at all. Maria received wonderful care there; everyone was professional and kind and compassionate. The differences existed, I guess, because of what the medical people were trying to do for our little girl.

At the first facility, they were trying to diagnose Maria's problem and find a treatment plan that would allow her to go home. She was surrounded by a mountain of medical equipment and a variety of personnel on a specialized wing where numerous patients suffered from a variety of somewhat similar neurological problems. The wing always seemed busy, and the mood of the visitors in the waiting area outside the wing ranged from excited optimism to serious concern and worry. During Maria's time there, in fact, I felt like we moved gradually from that optimistic extreme to the more somber extreme.

At the Hospice facility, by contrast, the hospital room itself seemed darker and smaller with less equipment and monitors and fewer personnel at the front desk, in the hallway, and in the room itself. The people there knew that Maria was not likely going to get better, and their sole task was to keep her comfortable and pain free and to provide her and her loved ones with whatever they needed. In fact, while the Hospice did provide a small waiting area near Maria's room with books, a large aquarium, and a television, it also provided a large, open, bright, family room at the end of the hall equipped with a kitchen area, a dining area, a game-and-puzzle area for small children, and a private sitting area where adults could talk quietly or pray. The staff members told us we could spend as much time there as we needed, and if we wanted to stay overnight with Maria, they would bring a cot into her room, so one of us could sleep right beside her. Thank you, Lord, for all of your provisions, on this day and always.

Thursday, January 21

The medical people at the hospital and at the Hospice facility had been giving Maria shots of morphine to lessen her pain, and they explained that morphine provided some immediate relief, but, unfortunately, that relief didn't last long. Thus, as the shot wore off, the patient soon required another shot to maintain the same level of relief.

So at some point, one of the doctors at the Hospice facility suggested that Maria have a minor operation to insert a device into her body that would allow her medical team to regularly give her pain medication directly through that device. In that way, Maria would not have to endure so many shots and would not have to experience the ups and downs of pain and relief and pain and relief again.

The idea made perfect sense, and because Barbara had had a similar device — a port — inserted for her IV treatments while she was undergoing treatment for her Hodgkin's lymphoma, I understood completely, and we all agreed that it was a good idea. Again, though, the experience was a bit surreal.

On this day, I accompanied Maria as they wheeled her from the Hospice wing on the fifth floor to the surgery wing in the basement. She was pretty much out of it, and we didn't communicate at all. Then, I sat in a waiting area as they performed the surgery, and I accompanied her back upstairs about an hour later when the procedure was completed. In many ways, the decision to insert the device for the morphine was a lot like the previous decisions to move Maria to Hospice, to sign the DNR form, and to remove her feeding tube. All these decisions seemed so counterintuitive; for instead of doing all we could to keep Maria alive with us, we were, in fact, doing all we could to painlessly hasten her departure and dispose of her earthly body.

How had we reached that point? Previously, we had so many plans and expectations for Maria, expectations that she, too, shared. We wanted to see her finish her master's degree in education, so that she could find a job as a full-time teacher. We wanted her to meet and fall in love with a good man who would love her and cherish her as much as we do. And we wanted to see her and this man get married and have children, our grandchildren. Now, none of that would happen for Maria. Instead, she was about to leave us. She would soon ascend into heaven to be with Jesus.

Once we had made all those decisions about moving Maria to Hospice, about signing the DNR form, about removing the feeding tube, and about inserting the morphine device, we also had to make a decision about what to do with Maria's body once she passed into heaven.

Over the years, Barbara and I had talked about this decision in relation to one another; we never expected we would have to make this decision for one of our children. And based on our family practices, we had two different experiences. On both sides of my family, we buried our loved ones in the cemetery, and we would visit the cemetery periodically to remember those loved ones.

Barbara's family also buried their loved ones, but since all of her immediate family members had moved from Long Island to upstate, we had never visited the graves of any of her ancestors during our marriage.

As we talked about the disposal of our bodies, Barbara didn't care for the cemetery burial and preferred the cremation approach. But she also said if I were to die first, she would do whatever I requested beforehand. Personally, I didn't have a strong preference one way or another, and I felt that if I died first, she could do whatever she wanted with my body, whatever she needed to help her through that experience.

Also, as strong believers in Jesus Christ, we believe that our human bodies are merely shells for our spiritual selves. Thus, we didn't see a significant difference between a burial or a cremation. In either case, when our spiritual self has left the body, the body will either deteriorate in the grave or be turned to ashes in the crematorium.

In the midst of making this decision about Maria, and even before we began to think about a wake or a funeral, one of the grief counselors at the Hospice facility approached us and asked if we wanted to consider donating Maria's body to the anatomical gift program, so that a medical student could study her body as part of that student's training.

Barbara, Katrina, and I were all immediately intrigued by the idea and in agreement about it. We were also familiar with the process because both of my parents had donated their bodies to the program. In Mom's case, her body was not used (and subsequently cremated) because of the infection in her body which caused her death. Dad's body was accepted for the program, and about a year after he passed, his ashes were returned to our family for burial next to Mom's ashes. In addition, our family was invited to attend a memorial event at a local cemetery where they remembered all the people who had donated their bodies to the program. I attended the ceremony with two of my sisters, and we were all impressed by the dignity of everyone involved. All of the medical students who had studied the bodies attended the ceremony and participated. In addition, the people in charge of the ceremony actually said that those who donated their bodies, so that future doctors could prepare for a career in medicine, were actually the first patients of those doctors.

Naturally, I later described the entire event to Barbara, so as we pondered the possibility for Maria's body, we agreed quickly and easily. Our Maria was always so passionate about teaching and always saw herself as a teacher, so we felt that by donating her body, she would not only be teaching a future medical professional about the human shell that God had given her, but Maria, in death, might also be helping that future doctor figure out what caused Maria's body to deteriorate so quickly and perhaps prevent a similar outcome for someone else.

That night, instead of going home, Barbara decided to stay with Maria and sleep on a cot next to her bed. Up to that point, none of us had stayed overnight with her. We typically stayed all day, every day with Maria. Barbara and I usually arrived between 8:00 and 9:00 each morning, and, then, we stayed with Maria until about 10:00 p.m. At that point, we went home to try and get a good night's sleep, so we could be available again the next day. And Katrina, who was working most days, would come by each evening and also visit on her off days. Looking back at that whole experience, it's easy to say we should have staggered our visits somewhat, or we should have taken turns staying with her overnight, but at the time, especially early on, we didn't know the seriousness of Maria's situation. We were still so hopeful day by day that she would recover from whatever was ailing her that we didn't feel the need to stay overnight, and Maria, in fact, always said that she'd be fine overnight without us because she had such a good rapport with the nurses who took care of her, and she had so much confidence in them. Those same nurses also encouraged us to go home each night; they promised to take good care of Maria, and they said they'd call us immediately if an emergency occurred. They also mentioned how some patients were able to sleep better knowing that their family members were also resting comfortably and would return early the next morning. In our case, at this point, we just knew Maria didn't have a lot of time left, and we simply did not want her to be alone again.

Friday, January 22

By the next morning, I had finished filling out the forms for Maria's body to be donated to science, and the experience was a bit odd. I was sitting in the kitchen area at the end of the hallway, probably about 50 yards away from Maria's room. She was about to leave us, and as her dad, I was giving the medical college permission to take her body when she left it to go to heaven to be with her Creator, Jesus Christ.

As I read through the forms and began to fill in the blanks, I had to recall her date and place of birth. Then, I had to jump 30 years ahead and provide her current address and place of employment. I also had to list the names of her family members and the names of her doctors.

In addition, I had to make a decision about what to do with Maria's ashes once the medical college finished with her body and had it cremated. We could either have her ashes buried at a local cemetery, or we could have them returned to us, so we could decide what we wanted to do with them. Barbara didn't really want the ashes, but she was okay with it if that's what Katrina and I wanted, which we did.

As we made the decision and signed the papers, we weren't sure what we would do with the ashes, and we still haven't permanently decided. In the years since Maria's ashes were returned to us, we have distributed some of them to multiple locations. First, Katrina took some of Maria's ashes to England because she and Maria had talked about taking that trip together. Then, we sprinkled some of them right here on our property where Maria grew up: in the backyard where she played on the swing set and, later, the trampoline; also in the side yard where we played wiffle ball and volleyball and soccer and, even later, where we hosted her high-school graduation party. We also spread some of her ashes near all of the schools she attended in town: her nursery school, her elementary school, and her high school. In addition, we brought some to Cape Cod which is where we had our last family vacation together during the summer of 2014 when we rented a place in Sandwich for a week. From that vacation, I especially remember the night when we made a small fire on the beach and sat out under the stars together and roasted marshmallows. I have so many wonderful family memories with our precious Maria.

  I should mention, too, how grateful we were for the family and friends who came to see us at the Hospice facility. I say "us" because most of our visitors did not have a chance to see Maria or say good-bye. Just as we had done at the previous hospital, we let everyone know ahead of time that Maria no longer wanted to see anyone besides immediate family, yet visitors arrived daily. They came to see us and to offer their support for us. They sat with us in the television room near the fish tank or in the big waiting room at the end of the hall. Naturally, they asked about Maria and brought cards, flowers, and food, and they offered to do anything we needed. Obviously, they couldn't provide the healing we sought for Maria, but their presence, their companionship, their conversations, and their prayers during those difficult days definitely helped us. We were surrounded by love and affection.

Saturday, January 23

I slept on the cot next to Maria's bed on Friday night during what became her last night here on Earth. We didn't know that at the time, of course, but, as I mentioned earlier, we no longer wanted Maria to be alone. Katrina and Barbara left the hospital around 10:00 on Friday night, and Maria seemed to sleep, for the most part, until about 5:00 a.m. on Saturday. At times during the night, I could hear her struggle to catch her breath. When that occurred, I sat up and watched intently because I felt she was about to leave us forever. In fact, I whispered to her, "Maria, it's okay. If you want to go home to Jesus now, you can. Don't worry about us. You will be at peace. You will be free from pain." This happened about four or five times, but she never let go completely. At that point, I began to wonder if she might be waiting for Barbara and Katrina to return.

At about 5:00 a.m., Maria became a bit restless, so I asked the nurse on duty if she could do anything for her. So during the next few hours, they tried different options. They repositioned her a bit, they suctioned fluid from her mouth, and they gave her a bit more pain medication and morphine. That hour between 5:00 and 6:00 a.m., before those treatments kicked in, seemed to be the toughest for Maria, so I folded up the cot and sat next to her: reading the Bible and singing old hymns to her.

I read the story of David praying for the first son he conceived with Bathsheba, the boy who died despite David's prayers. I also sang old church songs to her, songs such as "Great Is Thy Faithfulness"; "Be Thou Font of Every Blessing"; and "This Is My Story; This Is My Song."

Barbara and Katrina arrived around 10:30, and I thought that if Maria were waiting for them before she left us, she might do so soon after their arrival. An hour later, however, she still remained pretty much the same, so I began to think about going home for a while to take a nap since I had not slept that well on the cot and awoke often to check on Maria. I was hoping to get a few solid hours of sleep at home, so I could return later that day well rested and also spend Saturday night with Maria if needed.

So at about 11:30, I mentioned aloud to Barbara and Katrina that I was going to go home and sleep for a while. Almost immediately, Maria's breathing pattern changed drastically. What had been a slow, drawn-out, methodical pattern of air going in and out became somewhat rushed and fast-paced, almost as if Maria had become stressed at what I had said. Barbara and Katrina noticed it, too, and Barbara said, "You're not going anywhere."

I waited, and we all felt Maria's time had come. Her inhalations became even deeper, and when she exhaled, we began to hear the deep rattle that is often a sign of impending death. We gathered around her bed and waited. And waited.

She did not pass immediately. Her final hour was somewhat similar to what my dad had experienced just before he passed about a year and a half earlier. Barbara, Maria, Katrina, and I were all with Dad at the end, along with about 15 other family members. In Dad's case, we all had gathered around the bed in his bedroom at home, and we spoke to him, we prayed for him, and we cried together. In Maria's case, only Barbara, Katrina, and I surrounded Maria's bed. Naturally, we honored her request that no others be allowed in, not that it really mattered. At that hour on a Saturday morning, no visitors were in the waiting room for her.

As Maria moved closer to heaven in those final minutes, we noticed similarities between her farewell and my dad's farewell. Like Dad had done, Maria began to reach out her arms, and she seemed to be saying something, though we could not make out the words. In both cases, it was as if they were already gone from us in one respect and moving toward that next stage of life, toward eternity in heaven. Neither Dad nor Maria was looking at us any longer, but, instead, looking toward someone else, as if Jesus or other previously deceased family members were calling them home and welcoming them to their eternal resting places, the ones God had prepared for them so many years earlier.

Again, just like we had done previously, we spoke to Maria during this time. We told her how much we loved her, we told her it was okay to leave, and we said good-bye — with tears in our eyes and with an empty ache in our hearts. Our little girl and Katrina's big sister would no longer be with us physically.

Gradually, Maria's breathing slowed and became even more drawn out, so I called for the nurse to let her know we felt that the end was near. An older woman, she came immediately with her stethoscope and sat beside Maria and listened to her heartbeat. We watched silently as the nurse nodded her head to confirm what we all knew.

Within minutes, Maria's eyes closed fully for the last time. The rattling that we had heard previously with her breathing ceased, her arms remained at her side, motionless. And Maria died.

Barbara, Katrina, and I had all gathered on Maria's right side, and we were holding on to her and comforting one another. The nurse sat on Maria's left side, near her heart, and this nurse explained that she had to listen to Maria's silent heart for a full four minutes to confirm her final passing. We all watched and waited.

A small part of me rejoiced because I knew for sure that Maria was no longer in pain and that she truly rested finally in the arms of Jesus, her Creator; a much bigger part of me, however, selfishly cried for her loss. The little girl that I had welcomed into this world 30 years earlier was no longer with us.

After Maria breathed her final breaths on this earth — 12:25 p.m. — we left her hospital room relatively quickly. Knowing that Maria was no longer present in her human shell, Barbara did not want to stay there. She wanted to go home. By that point, Barbara's sister, Linda, had arrived, so she drove Barbara home while Katrina and I sat with Maria for a short time.

I'm not sure what motivated Katrina, but I knew I wanted to take one final look at Maria, and I wanted to thank God for all the joy that she brought into my life. I think I sat with her for about five to ten minutes, and Katrina stayed a bit longer. I think we both felt a little pressure to go be with Barbara who would be waiting for us at the house. I think we also felt a little pressure to go home because various family members were going to join us there. The people at the Hospice facility kindly offered to let us use the big room at the end of the hall — with kitchen appliances and a dining area and a waiting area — to greet people there if we wanted to, but I think we all wanted to go home, to the place where Maria grew up, to be surrounded by our family there.

  As mentioned previously, a good portion of my side of the family was already in town because our nephew Greg had organized a brunch birthday party for his wife and Maria's cousin, Renee, to celebrate her 30th birthday. Renee's family had previously offered to postpone the party when Maria's stay in the hospital began to drag on without a diagnosis, but they decided to go ahead with the party because Maria told her cousin and Renee's sister, Kyla, that it was okay to do so. In any event, my four sisters and other family members came to the house immediately, as did many members of Barbara's family. In their case, most of them had come to the area just because they had hoped to comfort us and, perhaps, see Maria one more time before she passed.

  As everyone entered our home, I could barely speak any words of consequence. I hugged everyone and thanked them for coming, and I even offered to hang up their coats for them. Otherwise, though, I could not say a word without getting all choked up, so I pretty much remained silent.

At one point, I tried to tell Rob, the husband of our niece Laura and the newest member of our family by marriage, how unfortunate it was that he hadn't had the time to really get to know Maria at all. "You didn't even know her," I said, and, then, I couldn't continue. Later, as I thought about the words that came out of my mouth, I felt like I had accused him of a wrongdoing, so I tried to explain myself, but again, I could barely speak. I was a mess.

In the midst of everyone's arrival, Greg showed up with a huge supply of food for everyone, and some neighbors had dropped off some food as well, so we all ate a late lunch/early dinner and tried to comfort one another. When I was finally able to speak normally again, I asked if anyone had a Maria story, and our nephew Danny recalled one immediately.

He said when he was about 12 years old, he played a baseball game in our area, and Barbara, Maria, Katrina, and I traveled to the field to watch the game. He said he had struck out and his team lost, but after the game, Maria, who was a few years younger, went up to him and said, "It's okay, Danny. We still love you." That was so typical of our little angel, trying to comfort others in the midst of their difficult situations. After everyone left, Katrina posted a notice on Facebook about Maria's passing, and Maria's friend Cate posted a similar message as well.

Katrina's post:

My sweet sister, Maria LaBate, went home to be with Jesus today after a short battle with cancer. Our lives will never be the same without her. Please know how much we appreciate everyone's love and support. She was so loved by so many. We will let you know of any service plans as they are scheduled.

Cate's post:

Can't thank each of you enough for praying. Maria went home today to be with the Lord after a short fight with cancer. Please keep her family in prayer.

Sunday, January 24

One of my morning rituals after I shower and dress is to go out the front door, walk down the driveway to the street, and retrieve our daily newspaper which is always folded into a large, plastic bag. As I walk down the driveway, which is only about 30 yards long, I get a feel for the day's weather and temperature, and I glance around the neighborhood to see if anything is different or unusual.

Normally, I see birds and squirrels scatter as I exit the house at about 7:30. Then, on some days, I see a neighbor or two out walking or jogging, and on other days, I may see someone driving to work, or I may see a school bus driving past our house and up the nearby hill. My short walk is comforting and reassuring because usually, the sun is coming up to my right, and the world seems orderly and normal. When I walked out the day after Maria's passing, however, I knew immediately that my world had changed.

No one else, of course, would have noticed the change. Sunday is always one of the quietest days of the week because no school buses are running, and most people probably sleep in a bit. Even those who get up and go to church on the Lord's day don't typically have to be up and out as early as they might during the week. So as I stepped down from our small front porch, nothing physical was out of the ordinary. The thought hit me, though, that this world was different because my first child was no longer in it.

The 30-foot pine tree that shades our driveway still stood tall and strong. The four townhouses to our right were still attached to our end unit. And the bright blue, winter sky overhead greeted me as it did most mornings, but Maria was no longer alive.

The girl who brightened our home for 18 years before going off to college had breathed her last. The girl who returned to our home for holiday visits and summer vacations would never visit again. And the young professional woman who called often with questions or with the desire to simply stay in touch would call me no more. My world was, indeed, different — less bright, less vibrant, and less alive.

As Barbara and I prepared for the day ahead, we had to make a decision about church. The night before, Barbara asked me if I thought I wanted to go. "Not if people will be there," I said seriously and somewhat lightheartedly. Of course, I knew people would be there, but I didn't think I would be ready to face anyone.

"What about you?" I asked.

"I think I'd like to go," she said, "but I won't go without you."

Later on that Sunday morning, after I had retrieved the newspaper, eaten breakfast, and showered and dressed, I had changed my mind. I didn't necessarily have a strong desire to go to church, to be surrounded by people, but if Barbara wanted to go, I could do that for her.

"Really?" she said when I told her. "It won't be too hard for you?"

"It might be hard," I admitted, "but maybe that's where we should be."

So we went to church, and in that building, we experienced the love of the body of Christ as I had never experienced it before.

We arrived around 10:15 for our 10:30 service. Many cars were already in the parking lot because our church offers Sunday School classes from 9:00 to 10:00. Thus, as Barbara and I entered the building and approached the hallway to the Sanctuary, I think most people were shocked to see us. Some people said "Hello" and "Good morning," but no one stopped us to offer condolences at that point, though we assumed most people had heard the news by then either through Facebook or the church's prayer chain.

Not exactly sure how to handle the situation, we entered the Sanctuary, and I suggested to Barbara that we sit in the back row just in case we wanted, or felt we needed, to leave the service early. I didn't realize it at that moment, but we were very close to where we sat on Christmas Eve with Maria, and we hadn't attended church since that night. We had spent the previous four Sundays at the hospital with Maria.

Barbara and I removed our coats and draped them over the chairs, and we were still standing when the informal procession began. People just came up to us and began hugging us. These were the people who knew us and loved us and who had watched Maria grow up in this church. Some of them were her friends or parents of her friends. Others had taught her in Sunday School or served as leaders of her youth group. All of them cared for us, and without any prompting or formal direction, they filed over and expressed their love and concern.

I began crying immediately and was speechless again. I remember taking off my glasses to wipe away my tears and silently hugging everyone. Most said they were so sorry or simply admitted that they didn't know what to say. No one really lingered to talk because a line had formed. Though none of us knew what to say, we all knew we had to hug one another, to silently express a human connection, an acknowledgment of loss and sadness and a fellowship of belief that Maria was already in heaven. Our hearts were breaking together, but Maria's was alive again as she rested comfortably, without pain, in the loving arms of Jesus, the God who created her 30 years earlier and now welcomed her home.

Epilogue

Katrina's Talk at Maria's Celebration Service

Hi. For those of you who don't know me, I am Maria's little sister, Katrina. As I thought about what to say to you all today, there were a lot of things that came to mind. A lot of them were the right things to say, the typical things you may expect to hear on a day like this. All of those things are, of course, true, and I'll get to them in a minute, but I also want to just take a second and say the real thing. The real thing is that as much as I am so glad and grateful that you are all here, I also hate that you are all here. I hate that this has to be taking place today, and that the fact that you are all here means my sister is no longer here with us on Earth. I wish we were gathering under different circumstances and that my words were simply in honor of Maria and not in memory of her. But, unfortunately, I cannot change what has happened. So, thank you for being here as we honor and remember my sister, Maria.

I can remember many times when Maria was sad, or our family was going through something difficult, and Maria would say to me, "Katrina, make me laugh. You are always good at making me feel better." So, today, my goal is to try and bring a little bit of joy and laughter to this day which, on the surface, seems anything but joyful. I can't make any promises, but my goal is to bring a smile to your faces today as we remember Maria and her sweet smile. I'll do my best to stop crying because I think it's probably easier to make people laugh when I'm not standing up her crying. But once again, I can't promise that.

The last time I remember trying to make her laugh was in the hospital. She was having a rough day, and I tried to think of something to take her mind off her discomfort. I said to her, "Maria, try to think of the time when I made you the maddest." She quickly laughed and came up with something very easily. So I like to think that maybe I had to make her so mad all those years ago, so that I could help bring a smile to her face just a few weeks ago when smiles were much harder to come by.

My sister was two and a half years older than I, and we used to joke about how she had to put up with our parents alone before I came along, and when she left for college, it was my turn. I'm sure there were plenty of times growing up when she wished she was a little bit older during those two and a half years without me, so she could have really enjoyed and taken full advantage of the peace and quiet that came along with being an only child, especially once she found out who her sister was going to be and that peace and quiet was not always my strong suit. If only she knew what she was in for.

Maria had a soft, peaceful, and independent spirit about her, and I know I drove her crazy sometimes, but I think we learned a lot from each other. We helped each other find areas of ourselves that were not our natural default modes. I tried to help bring out her silly and carefree side, and she showed me what it meant to just be still. As I got older, I started to see how nice it could be to just be alone and experience quiet. I started to realize why sometimes she would just disappear all of a sudden and go up to her room to be alone for a while. She knew what she needed to do in order to take care of herself. She had mastered the Irish goodbye at a young age. Looking back, I think she had it right all along. Sometimes, people can be tiring, and you just need to get away for a little while and recharge. She showed me how to do that.

For those of you who know Maria, you know how much she loved a good schedule. She always wanted to know what the plan was. I remember growing up, Maria would often ask my mom what was for dinner before we left for school in the morning. Unfortunately, that's not how things worked in our house. Dinner was more of a last-minute decision. Personally, I pretty much hate when my schedule is booked up and a plan is set in stone, and I could not always understand Maria's need for detailed order. I probably could have done a better job at trying to understand that side of her, but if there were ever a time that I wished I could have made a plan for her, it would be during the last month of her life.

Throughout the 30 days that she was in the hospital, there were two things in particular that were the most upsetting to her. The first was when she found out she would not be able to continue with graduate school this semester. She had just finished up her first semester in her master's in literacy for elementary education. She loved her classes and was so excited to be on a track towards her dream and passion of being a teacher, and now that plan was being put on hold.

The second thing was when she knew school was not an option, all she wanted was to be able to go home. She would ask me if we could just bring her home even for a day and promised she would come back to the hospital. She was so frustrated with being in the hospital and not knowing the next step. It broke my heart to not be able to give her an answer and a plan to make her better, and at the very least, to grant her what should be a simple request: to just go home. I wish there could have been a plan we could have made to restore her back to health. But God had a different plan for Maria, and despite the amazing care of all her doctors and nurses who took wonderful care of her as well as us, God's plan involved bringing her to His home in Heaven.

While she never got to have her classroom here on Earth, I hope she knows that she was always a teacher. In her last days, she taught us what it meant to be kind. In the middle of her pain, she never stopped asking people how they were and thanking everyone who came into her room even if they were there to do a test or take her down for a procedure. She taught us what it meant to be brave as she faced the scary unknown with such poise and elegance. And she taught us to love and to be grateful for one another. She was grateful when the four of us were together and grateful that we could cry together, laugh together, or just sit quietly together. I will forever cherish our last days as a family of four. We were all together when she took her final breaths, and she pulled her final Irish goodbye and left the room for the last time, this time entering into her eternal home where she will experience the ultimate peace and healing that we could not give her here.

I hope she is busy making perfect schedules, filled with things she loves, and teaching children maybe whose parents are still here on Earth, and I know she will take good care of them. Heaven will be her forever classroom where she will be everything God created her to be for all eternity. I know she will be preparing the way for us when we will join her again one day and be reunited as a family. Until then, we will keep her spirit with us every day. We will try to remember to be kind, to be brave, to love, and to be grateful for the time we have with one another here on Earth.

So thank you again for taking time today and putting Maria on your schedules. For those of you who knew Maria personally, that means that at one time or another, you made it onto her schedule, and I hope you know that shows just how important you were to her. If you never had the chance to meet my sister, thank you so much for your love and support for our family, and I hope you get a glimpse today of how special she was, and may her story continue to touch others for a very long time. Thank you.

I love you, Maria.

Jim's Talk at Maria's Celebration Service

Good morning. This is a glorious day. Yes, it's a bit cold out there, but this is still a glorious day.

On behalf of our entire, extended family, we thank you all for coming. We definitely appreciate all the love and support and prayers and meals and acts of kindness that we have received, and we are so grateful for all the generous gifts you have made to Compassion International on Maria's behalf. The body of Christ has definitely surrounded us in these last few weeks.

As you can see from that PowerPoint program, we have a tradition in our family of photographing our children in front of the Christmas Tree each year. That tradition began in 1985 when Maria was born on December 21, and I have always said that she was the best Christmas gift I ever received.

And as we look at those photos, we can see the remarkable growth that took place in her life: from the tiny baby in the infant carrier to the little girl holding a small purse to the smiling adolescent excited over a new sweater to the beautiful, young woman we all remember today.

Unfortunately, we never got to take Maria's picture on Christmas Day this past December. She wasn't feeling well that morning, and later that evening, when other signs indicated a serious problem, we called an ambulance, which rushed her to the hospital. Sadly, as Katrina mentioned earlier, Maria never came home to us again. Instead, she went home to Jesus. She spent the last 30 days of her life in two different hospitals.

Since Maria's passing, many people have said that at age 30, she was much too young to die, and from a selfish and earthly perspective, these people are right. But when I look back on all those wonderful years with Maria, I feel so blessed to have had the opportunity to share them with her.

In fact, if God had come to me in 1985, and said, "Jim, I have a beautiful, little girl I'd like you to watch over and take care of for 30 years; would you be willing to do so?" I know I would have eagerly said, "Absolutely."

And as I look back on those 30 years, I remember lots of big days and special moments like graduations from grade school and high school and college. I remember Maria winning medals at gymnastics meets when she was in middle school, playing tennis in high school, and acting in a play in college. But what I most fondly remember are the day-to-day pleasures of life with Maria.

Before she started school, I remember stacking little, plastic cups with her from biggest to smallest and then laughing with her as she knocked the whole pile over. I remember reading to her before bedtime; not surprisingly, the story *The Giving Tree* by Shel Silverstein was one of her favorites. I remember playing soccer and wiffle ball in the side yard. I remember eating popcorn on the couch as we watched *The Little Mermaid* and *Beauty and the Beast*. Later, when Maria was a bit older, the two of us would make a date to go see IMAX or 3D movies together. I remember teaching her to drive and parallel park. I remember visiting colleges with her and talking to her about her career plans. Obviously, I could go on and on with numerous stories and lots of details, but I won't. Thirty years are not enough, but they are 30 years I will always treasure.

So, yes, we are all struggling today because we all wanted more time with Maria. But today is Maria's final commencement ceremony. She has graduated from this life, and she has entered the eternal resting place that Jesus Christ intended for her all along, the one He had in mind for her when He knit her bones together in Barbara's womb over 30 years ago.

So as we look at the photo of the LaBate Christmas Tree from 2015, we do not see Maria; we see only the tree. But as we look at that solitary tree, we know Maria was with us because we all have so many memories of her in our hearts and in our minds. And just as we have the empty crucifix right here on the wall to remind us that Jesus gave His life for us and rose from the dead, we can look at the solitary Christmas Tree and remember that, yes, Maria was with us, but now, she, too, has risen from the dead to join her Creator in heaven.

And I sincerely believe that's the only way we can get through a difficult time like this. We must know and believe, as Maria did from a young age, that Jesus created us, that He has a master plan for our lives, that He came to Earth and died for us, and that if we submit ourselves to Him, as Maria did wholeheartedly, we, too, will spend eternity with Him in heaven.

So thank you, Jesus, for the gift of Maria's life. She is your little girl, and today, we celebrate her life and rejoice that she is back in your loving arms. This is, indeed, a glorious day.

Barbara's Talk at Maria's Celebration Service

Thank you so much for being here with us celebrating Maria's life and honoring our Lord and Savior Jesus Christ.

It is inconceivable; it is incomprehensible; it is unspeakable what has happened to all of us, and our lives will never be the same. But we can be assured that Maria is not missing us because we are there with her, now that she is out of the dimension of time and free from sin. Our hearts ache because we are still living in the dimension of time, but she is completely whole. Maria is a shining light and even more so now because she is restored and out of pain. She is loving on children and adults. She is smiling at everyone she sees. I couldn't be happier for her while, at the same time, I am missing her terribly. But, for now, Maria is cheering us on with the great cloud of witnesses, so that we fulfill our destinies in Christ Jesus.

Deuteronomy 31:6 says, "Be strong and courageous. Do not be afraid or terrified . . . for the Lord your God goes with you; He will never leave you nor forsake you."

From early on, Maria has been strong in her love for the Lord and for people. In 1990, when Maria was five, she asked us if she could sing a song at the LaBate and Zuccaro Christmas gatherings. The chorus to the song goes like this:

Christmas isn't Christmas
till it happens in your heart.
Somewhere deep inside you
is where Christmas really starts.
So give your heart to Jesus,
you'll discover when you do,
That it's Christmas,
really Christmas for you.

1 Peter 3:3-4 says, "Your beauty should not come from outward adornment . . . Instead, it should be that of your inner self, the unfading beauty of a gentle and quiet spirit, which is of great worth in God's sight."

Maria has a gentle spirit, a beautiful smile, and only kind words for others. She is a teacher, an encourager, and an overcomer. I have to admit that, at times, we got frustrated when she was in teaching mode. Sometimes we just wanted her to be our daughter and sister, but it was just in her DNA to teach. I'm sorry, Maria, for our impatience.

During her elementary and middle-school years when she made a really close friend, God often moved that friend away. In her sadness, Maria learned to adapt and continued to reach out to others to either encourage or be encouraged. Somehow, she knew of her need for both.

2 Corinthians 4: 6-7 says, "For God, who said, 'Let light shine out of darkness,' made His light shine in our hearts to give us the light of the knowledge of the glory of God in the face of Christ. But we have this treasure in jars of clay to show that this all-surpassing power is from God and not from us."

Maria lived with chronic pain in her spine for five years. Recently, she dealt with the disappointment of not having her own classroom. And, yet, she continued to adapt and make the best of her life. I believe the world is her classroom and that we all have been and will continue to be the beneficiaries of her example of living her life for Jesus.

Isaiah 12:2 says, "Surely, God is my salvation; I will trust and not be afraid. The Lord, the Lord is my strength and my song; He has become my salvation."

The message that Maria's life so exemplified is simply this: "Jesus loves me, this I know, for the Bible tells me so. Little ones to him belong. We are weak, but He is strong." Maria lives for Jesus, and she wants each and every one of us to fulfill the destiny that God put in us before we were born and to embrace Jesus as our Lord and Savior because He loves us so much, and He knows how much we need Him.

I, too, love you, Maria and am grateful for the time that God gave you to me.

I would like to invite everyone to share an encouraging word for us, a story of your own, or a story about Maria. We have index cards on the guest-book table and in the Fellowship Hall for your convenience. It would be a blessing to us if you took a little time to fill one out, so we can make a memory book of our precious daughter and sister. Thank you ahead of time.

Reflections

Four Words to Ease the Pain

I've been thinking about death lately. My mother-in-law passed away at age 90, my sister's mother-in-law passed away at age 98, and we attended their memorial services. The nine-year anniversary of our daughter's death at age 30 has passed, and my wife and I recently attended a support group for parents who have lost children. Thus, I find myself contemplating the difference between the passing of a senior citizen and the passing of a young person.

The passing of an elderly person seems to be easier on the immediate family because the deceased had lived a long, full life, and in some cases, her passing may bring to an end any discomfort or struggles that may have plagued her. Her loss, naturally, is still difficult for the loved ones left behind, but they might be able to console themselves with their memories, and they might be grateful for their shared experiences. The loss of a young person like our Maria, however, is usually more difficult. Maria did not get to live a "long, full life." She didn't fall in love and get married, she didn't have children, and she never had the opportunity to fully use the gifts God had given her.

Yes, the passing of a young person may be a blessing of sorts if that young person had "discomfort or struggles" of her own, problems that may have intensified or persisted interminably. And while the loved ones left behind might also console themselves with memories or be grateful for shared experiences, they might, in addition, feel cheated out of the anticipated family relationships that never occurred and the career activities that they never witnessed. As a result, the mourning for a young person may last longer and be more challenging.

All these thoughts came to my mind when Barbara and I sat in that support group with other still-grieving parents, all members of a unique community we never sought to join. As we shared our stories of loss and adjustment to that loss, we discussed some commonalities.

Generally speaking, those who mourn with us really don't know what to say. Most of us have experienced that difficulty. Trying to comfort the parents of a deceased child is likely impossible. After all, parents are not supposed to bury their children, so almost anything that anyone might say will likely not be comforting.

"I'm sorry" is a good start.

"I can't even imagine . . ." is a sincere follow-up. Anything else, unfortunately, may be hard to accept, especially in the days immediately following the child's passing.

"She's in a better place."

"God wanted her in heaven."

"She's no longer suffering."

"She wouldn't want you to be sad or depressed."

While all these statements may be true, as still-mourning survivors, we're not quite ready to accept the truth just yet. In fact, we may never fully understand or adjust in a way or on a schedule that others expect.

Please give us time. Give us a little space. Don't rush us back to a world that is so different because it no longer includes our precious child.

Just be with us. Be available. And don't be afraid to say our child's name. Yes, we might cry. We might be sad. We might be quiet. But we want others to remember her. We don't want to let her go — ever. We want to hold on. She's a part of us, a forever part.

When our Maria passed, I had one old friend come to see me within days, and he said four simple words that not only made me cry, but they also allowed me the opportunity to talk about my first child.

Kevin and his wife attended our church when Maria was born, and we often socialized together with other young couples. In fact, Kevin and Karen babysat for Maria overnight once when she was two, when Barbara and I had a chance for a short, work-related getaway. So Kevin knew Maria when she was young, but he and Karen moved away a few years later, so they didn't have the chance to watch her grow up. Sure, we tried to stay in touch, and we visited periodically, too, but the three-hour trip became more of a challenge when our Katrina arrived and when Kevin and Karen began to raise children of their own.

Thus, I was pleasantly surprised to hear Kevin's voice when he called. Obviously, he, too, said he was sorry, but he also said he wanted to drive over to see me that same day. He claimed he had a work meeting nearby, but I still don't believe that story. I believe he sincerely just wanted to be there for me, and his story made it easier for me to say, "Yes. C'mon over."

And after he greeted me and hugged me in our living room, he didn't offer any advice or recite any of the normal platitudes. Instead, he simply said four words: "Tell me about Maria."

He used her name. And he gave me the opportunity to talk about my precious first-born. Yes, I cried — often — as I told Kevin about the grown-up version of the little girl he once knew. I told him about Maria's sincere love for Jesus, about her passion for tennis and reading and writing, about her love for children, and about her desire to teach. I told him, too, about her struggles and her failures and about her final 30 days in the hospital when an undiagnosed case of breast cancer spread to her brain and took her away, despite her own plea that "I'm too young to die."

So, yes, nine years have passed since Kevin visited me and allowed me to talk about Maria. And while I am not by any means an expert on grief or on how to comfort others, I do know that on that day, in our living room, Kevin's four words brought me a certain comfort, a comfort that I recall fondly as I think of my old friend and as I remember our dear, precious Maria.

Does God Answer Our Prayers?

If you've ever been to a church service or listened to a Christian radio station, you may have heard a testimony like the following: "Our child was seriously ill, and the doctors gave us an extremely negative prognosis, but we did not give up. We prayed and prayed, and everyone we knew prayed for a healing, and God answered our prayers. Our child recovered and is healthy and strong today. God is good. Praise God!"

I, too, have heard similar versions of this story on numerous occasions. As a result, I have faith in God, and I praise Him for His healing powers and His answers to prayers. About nine years ago, however, I experienced this story with a distinctly different outcome.

On her 30th birthday (December 21), our older daughter, Maria, complained of a terrible headache, what she imagined to be a migraine, though she had never experienced migraines before. She visited her doctor, but her pain persisted. Days later, we brought her to an emergency facility; again, the treatment offered did not help. On Christmas Day, she lost her vision in one eye, so we called an ambulance and brought her to the hospital. Within 30 days, Maria was gone.

Initially, the hospital doctors were puzzled by Maria's problems, and they described her as a "diagnostic dilemma." After numerous tests and procedures, they finally figured out that she had breast cancer and that it had spread to her brain. By then, however, the damage had been done, and they could do nothing to save her. Maria is now in heaven.

But wait. That can't be true. We prayed for her healing. Everyone prayed for her recovery. Yet Maria did not survive. So did God not answer our prayers? This is the question I ponder today.

In John 15:7, Jesus said, "If you remain in me and my words remain in you, ask whatever you wish, and it will be given you."

Earlier, in John 14:14, Jesus also said, "You may ask me for anything in my name, and I will do it." Thus, I have to admit I am puzzled by the outcome in Maria's case.

In my quest to understand, I recall other similar stories of loss in the Bible. David, described as a "man after God's own heart" (1 Samuel 13:14), also endured a difficult situation with his child. The son that David had as a result of his adulterous relationship with Bathsheba became seriously sick. Naturally, David "pleaded with God for the child" (2 Samuel 12:16). Unfortunately, the boy died, and the prophet Nathan explained that the boy's death was a punishment for David's sin with Bathsheba (2 Samuel 12:7-19).

The book of Job chronicles another tragic loss of life. Regarding Job, God says: "There is no one on earth like him; he is blameless and upright, a man who fears God and shuns evil" (Job 1:8). The text also says that Job often prayed for his seven sons and three daughters. Yet, in that same chapter, we read that all of Job's children died in the midst of a terrible storm. In this case, though, Job was not being punished for his sin. Instead, God allowed Satan to test Job's faithfulness by taking away his children and his possessions (Job 1:9-19).

Finally, in the New Testament, I recall the story of Lazarus. When this friend of Jesus became sick, his two sisters, Mary and Martha, sent word to Jesus regarding the situation. Instead of rushing to see Lazarus or healing him from afar, however, Jesus stayed where He was for two more days, and Lazarus died. At that point, Jesus said to his disciples, "Lazarus is dead, and for your sake, I am glad I was not there, so that you may believe. But let us go to him" (John 11:14-15). Obviously, Jesus knew He was going to raise Lazarus from the dead, but Lazarus had to die first for that to happen. In a similar way, Jesus Himself offered His life on the cross to prove His power over death through His Resurrection. So the death of Lazarus and the death of Jesus both serve a greater purpose, a purpose that is not initially understood by those who were close to the one who died.

So what happened in Maria's case? Am I being punished, like David, for my sins? That's a possibility since I have sinned often. Or is God testing me, and others who loved Maria, just as he tested Job? Again, that's a possibility, and we are all dealing with broken hearts and pondering our loss. Or is Maria's passing, like the passing of Lazarus, serving a greater purpose, one well beyond our earthly understanding? This possibility, too, exists, and we may not learn the answer until we ourselves pass into eternity.

So what have I learned from all of these stories and others like them? I have realized that God doesn't have the same earthly plan, a one-size-fits-all plan, for everyone. Just because God often answers prayers and heals some people doesn't necessarily mean He's going to treat all others in the same way. Rather, God answers our prayers in numerous ways, and He has a unique plan for each of us: "For I know the plans I have for you," declares the Lord, "plans to prosper you and not to harm you, plans to give you hope and a future" (Jeremiah 29:11).

Yes, we lost Maria, just as David lost his son, just as Job lost his children, and just as Mary and Martha lost their brother for a short time before God brought him back to life. Rather than look at Maria's passing from a purely earthly perspective, however, I must take the eternal view. I must trust that God has plans to give me "hope and a future," a heavenly future that will include Maria and an eternal future that will not end in death.

So does God answer our prayers? Of course He does — In His time and in His way. And for that, I am grateful.

The Author . . .

Jim LaBate spent the final 20 years of his career as a writing specialist in The Writing Center at Hudson Valley Community College in Troy, New York. There, he received the Chancellor's Award for Excellence in Teaching in 2019.

Originally from Amsterdam, New York, Jim earned his bachelor's degree in English from Siena College in Loudonville, New York, and his master's degree, also in English, from The College of Saint Rose in Albany, New York.

Jim spent his entire career as either a teacher or a writer. He taught physical education as a Peace Corps Volunteer in Golfito, Costa Rica, for two years. He taught high-school English for 10 years (one year at Vincentian Institute in Albany, New York, and nine years at Keveny Memorial Academy in Cohoes, New York). Then, he worked for 10 years as a writer for Newkirk Products in Albany, New York, before moving to HVCC.

Jim lives in Clifton Park, New York, with his wife, Barbara; they have two daughters: Maria and Katrina.

Previous Works

Let's Go, Gaels — a novella — tells the story of one week in the life of a 12-year-old boy. The story takes place in a Catholic school in upstate New York in 1964. As the week begins, the narrator is thinking about a speech he has to give in English class on Friday, a big basketball game on Saturday, and a trip to the movies on Saturday night. During the week, however, something happens that changes his life — and his outlook on life — forever. The event moves him further away from his innocent boyhood and closer to his eventual maturity as a man.

Mickey Mantle Day in Amsterdam — another novella — is also about growing up. This particular story focuses on baseball and on baseball's biggest name in the 1950s and the 1960s. The story takes place during the summer of 1963 when Mantle is on the disabled list, recovering from a broken foot. When his car breaks down near the "Rug City," the 12-year-old narrator and his dad stop to help, and Mantle's Amsterdam adventure begins. By the time it ends, 24 hours later, both the narrator and the reader have learned a valuable lesson.

Things I Threw in the River: The Story of One Man's Life — In this novel, the first-person narrator lives near the Mohawk River in upstate New York during the 1950s, '60s, '70s, and '80s. He tells a series of related stories about what he threw into the river and why. The first story concerns an incident that occurs when the narrator is four years old, and the final story occurs in 1988 when he is 37. That final story is the most dramatic of all, takes up 50% of the novel, and is based on a real incident.

My Teacher's Password: A Contemporary Novel — Tom Sullivan is a 21-year-old college student, and he's in love with his creative writing professor — as well he should be. Margaret Cavellari is hot! She looks like a cross between Catherine Zeta-Jones and Penelope Cruz. Okay, so no one is really that hot, but Margaret is close. In addition, she's kind. She's funny. She's interesting. And she's a great teacher. So when Tom accidentally discovers her computer password, what will he do? Will he read her e-mail? Will he look at her pictures and her word processing files? Will he go into her gradebook? Naturally, Tom Sullivan is curious. But is he also stupid? Of course he is. Read all about Tom's computer adventures in this contemporary novel.

Writing Is Hard: A Collection of Over 100 Essays — This book serves as an alternative to the traditional writing handbook which typically attempts to explain the entire writing process or to address thoroughly all areas of punctuation, grammar, and usage. Such a text can be overwhelming and intimidating. Instead, the author uses each essay to focus on only one small aspect of writing with the hope that the reader will walk away with the key idea, one that can be easily remembered and implemented. Each essay is a self-contained lesson of about 700 words written in an informal, conversational style.

Streets of Golfito — This novel focuses on two individuals who meet in Golfito, Costa Rica, in 1974. Jim (Diego) is a 22-year-old Peace Corps Volunteer from upstate New York, and he has been assigned to introduce sports other than soccer to the young people. By contrast, Lilli is a shy, beautiful, 17-year-old Costa Rican girl who wants to learn English and escape her small town, a banana port on the Pacific side near the Panamanian border. In alternating chapters, the first third of the book shows these two characters growing up in their respective countries. Then, after they meet, Lilli experiences a tragedy that will drastically change her life, and Jim does all he can to help her survive and thrive in her new circumstances.

Order Form

Name _____

Address _____

City _____ State _____ Zip _____

Let's Go, Gaels $5.95 x ____ copies = _____

Mickey Mantle Day
   in Amsterdam $7.95 x ____ copies = _____

Things I Threw
   in the River $9.95 x ____ copies = _____

My Teacher's
   Password $9.95 x ____ copies = _____

Writing Is Hard $19.95 x ____ copies = _____

Streets of Golfito $19.95 x ____ copies = _____

Our Sweet Maria $19.95 x ____ copies = _____

Postage & Handling $5.00 x ____ copies = _____

                                        Subtotal _____

New York residents add appropriate sales tax _____

                                            Total _____

Please enclose a check for your order and mail to:

57 Carriage Road
Clifton Park, New York 12065-7503
518-383-2254
www.MohawkRiverPress.com

www.ingramcontent.com/pod-product-compliance
Lightning Source LLC
Chambersburg PA
CBHW071907290426
44110CB00013B/1308